How to avoid DIY

By Cliff Parker and published by New English Library

HOW TO AVOID YOUR GARDEN
HOW TO AVOID FLYING
HOW TO AVOID SEX
HOW TO AVOID SLIMMING
HOW TO AVOID DO-IT-YOURSELF

ABOUT THE AUTHOR

Cliff Parker, known to his friends as Jericho because his walls keep tumbling down, is the holder of several do-it-yourself records. The two most talked about in demolition circles are the Most-Expensive-Bathtap-Washer-Replacement (for which he could have bought a whole new bath) and the Least-Longstanding-Set-of-Bookshelves (thirty-five seconds, if you must know).

He lives in Amersham, Buckinghamshire, in a characterful (i.e. roofless) little house, and has a wife and two children, all of whom have been struck by collapsing wall fittings and the *Complete Works of Shakespeare*.

How to avoid DIY

Cliff Parker

Illustrated by Barry Robson

NEW ENGLISH LIBRARY

ACKNOWLEDGEMENT

Grateful thanks to Polycell Products Limited for providing the information freely misused in Chapter One.

A New English Library Original Publication, 1984.

First NEL Paperback Edition October 1984

NEL Books are published by
New English Library,
Mill Road, Dunton Green,
Sevenoaks, Kent.
Editorial office: 47 Bedford Square, London WC1B 3DP

Made and printed in Great Britain by Cox & Wyman Ltd, Reading

0 450 05740 2

To
JOHN HARVEY
without whom the world would be a duller place.
Even if it did last longer.

CONTENTS

How to avoid DIY

INTRODUCTION

One of the truly startling social phenomena of the past thirty years is the growth of do-it-yourself. And an excellent idea it is, too. If you like that sort of thing.

For a modest outlay, you can turn a slum into a little palace. For even less, you can turn a little palace into a slum. You can fill otherwise blank and boring evenings and weekends with meaningful and creative activity.

But some of us, for example the majority of married men, can fill our evenings and weekends quite well without knocking things down or knocking things up. Some of us are just not equipped for DIY, mentally or physically. Some of us are not endowed with the trueness of eye or sureness of hand necessary for the full realisation of our potential as home handymen. Some of us are – how can we put it? – bone idle.

DIY is not compulsory. Not yet. But we are faced with massive social and commercial pressures to improve our humble but perfectly satisfactory abodes. If we are not standing at the top of a ladder, drill in hand and wondering what the hell to do with it, we do not love our wives. We are failing in our social and domestic responsibilities. We are not Men.

Meanwhile our otherwise loving wives are prompted by the same pressures to force us – unskilled, unenergetic and unwilling as we are – into unfamiliar, exhausting and often dangerous areas of activity.

This book sets out to examine the social and economic implications of DIY, and to provide a basic manual of guerrilla tactics for fighting back. If it seems to take a male chauvinistic attitude, it's merely because it takes a male chauvinistic attitude. You can't please 'em all.

So go to it, lads. Remember the stirring slogan:

BOTCHERS OF THE WORLD UNITE –
YOU'VE GOT NOTHING TO LOSE BUT YOUR SPRAINS.

And if all else fails, faint.

CHAPTER ONE

Love and Marriage

Do-it-yourself is 'more a labour of love than a chore . . .a practical way of expressing basic emotions of loving and caring . . .a visible way of working constructively for the good of the marriage . . .'

Gad, I wish I'd thought of that. It's a quote from the first of three reports by the DIY manufacturers Polycell*, analysing the home improvement market. Excellent stuff it is, too, illustrating the ever-increasing part DIY plays in our lives and going a long way to explain how the husbands of the world got into this mess in the first place.

It's the women, you see. Not that nobody suspected it before, but it's nice to have it in writing.

This first report in 1978 included an analysis of group discussion among handyman husbands. 'As prime instigators to get things moving, [the wives'] contribution was never in dispute,' says the report. 'The wife not only decides what is to be done, but has the final say in choice of materials and colour schemes.'

Not that nobody would have guessed, but read on: 'The physical work is generally seen as the man's duty and once it is under way the wife generally steers well clear of the area.'

From there, misplaced male chauvinism is allowed to take over. Husbands in the discussion groups felt they could get on better on their own, and often quoted cases of jobs bungled by their wives which they, in their macho way, were proud to put right.

Oo's a clever boy, den?

The second Polycell report, published in 1981, featured an interview with 500 wives. Though it contained some quite terrifying statistics on the women's role as subversives, burrowing their way

* Registered trade mark of Polycell Products Ltd.

into their husbands' leisure time and peace of mind, there were hopeful signs of a growing resistance movement among the men.

Noting that 'on the whole, it seems that wives are the ones who push for home improvements,' the report observes: 'Their enthusiasm is not spontaneously shared by the majority of husbands, who need some encouragement.' What a nice way of putting it.

Nearly two-thirds of the wives said they had to prod their menfolk to get on with jobs around the home. One-fifth claimed that their husbands were not even interested in DIY.

However, after being 'prodded' (and the mind boggles about what that entailed), 56 per cent of the husbands got on with the jobs. 'Willingly,' said the report.

Now – and here's the crafty bit – eight out of ten wives said their husbands' jobs were finished up to professional standard. And nearly two-thirds gave them credit for being neat and tidy workers.

Watch it, lads. Once you get a reputation like that . . .

Having dished out the praise, six out of ten wives felt they could do jobs just as well as their husbands. Good girls. Don't just stand there: get on with it.

One-fifth of the wives – presumably with the non-interested husbands – said they'd rather get a professional in to do the job.

That's no shame, lads: just an acknowledgement of the firm stand you've taken. Keep it up. Half of humanity is relying on you.

Let's have a bit more of the first Polycell report. Sheer romance, it is:

'Taking the theme further – the labour of love – there are undoubtedly deepseated emotional implications for home improvement.

'Making the house more comfortable for the wife makes for a happier home life. A conspicuous act of home improvement gives the wife the opportunity to show off what "we" have done to the house.

'In any given year a major piece of home improvement can literally help cement a marital relationship . . .'

Mills and Boon should hear about this.*

There's always someone ready to take the romance out of things, though. A British psychologist observed that excessive indulgence in DIY on the part of the husband might not be an indication of his devotion to his beloved. It could mean that he can't stand the sight of her and is taking on jobs around the house to keep out of her way.

How about that for a get-out? You'd be hard put to find another excuse half so romantic:

'Darling, I'd be *delighted* to paper the ceiling,' he said, his steel-and-whipcord muscles rippling under the rough fabric of his working shirt. 'But I love you too much to have you out of my sight for so long'.

'Oh, Charles!' she gasped, her bosom heaving as the full implication of his words dawned on her. 'I never realised you cared so much! How could I allow such trivial and material considerations

* STOP PRESS. Even as we write, the Polycell Report for 1984 lands on the doormat. The news is that DIY surges ahead yet again, with the British market alone doubling from £1 billion to £2 billion since 1978. Eek!

to come between us? How could I impose such monotonous and menial tasks upon so fine and noble a mind?'

'Sit down on the settee, my sweet. Open a six-pack and watch "World of Sport". Forget I ever mentioned anything so sordid, and I'll get on with it myself.'

And so the marital bonds are cemented as the loving wife, still quivering with emotion, climbs the ladder and sets to work, feeling his passionate gaze burning through the thin nylon of her overall as she applies herself eagerly to her task.

The passionate gazing doesn't go on all the time, of course. Only during the commercial breaks. And once the late results have been announced, the husband's eyes may close altogether. This is further proof of his gentlemanly instincts – he can't bear to watch his loved one exerting herself.

CHAPTER TWO

Taking the Strain

The strain that excessive or ill-advised DIY activity can put on a marriage is not an invention of the comedy scriptwriter: it's happening all the time in real life.

Every week, in happy little family homes, something falls off, bends, buckles, breaks, dissolves, crumbles, collapses, bursts into flame or explodes.

Most of the cases go unreported: accidents will happen, after all. Often the only evidence of a disaster, apart from a pile of rubble and timber where once stood a kitchen or living room, is the battered appearance of the person responsible.

The person responsible is usually a husband dedicated to the cause of home improvements. And if the battering was not inflicted by the falling masonry, it was inflicted after the dust had settled by a wife who was not entirely pleased with the outcome of her loved one's efforts. Women are funny that way: if there's one thing that upsets them, it's the house falling down about their ears.

Frank Spencer, cack-handed anti-hero of the television series 'Some Mothers Do 'Ave 'Em', has millions of viewers in hysterics as he moves confidently from one disaster to another. But, for the one fictional Frank, there are millions of real-life home-wreckers spread throughout the world, husbands who indulge in do-it-yourself to the point of fanaticism.

Sometimes the disasters are big enough, or have been going on long enough, for a distraught wife to call a halt with the words: 'It's either do-it-yourself – or me!' And sometimes the husband is really shattered by the ultimatum: nobody knows how much he's going to miss her . . .

A British husband who couldn't make up his mind was divorced by his wife on the grounds of cruelty and desertion.

The divorce court heard that George – it had to be George – couldn't decide whether or not to paper the walls of his home, so he asked the local priest. The priest advised the used of good old-fashioned distemper, he being a good old-fashioned priest, 31 years older than the husband and his spiritual adviser since he was a lad.

George's wife wanted a water heater. He wasn't sure whether it was a good idea or not. So he asked the priest. And so it went on.

George's wife, Doris – it had to be Doris – always consulted him about anything that needed doing, though why she bothered was never made clear. Sometimes George would give her a definite yes, but then doubts would set in and he would call round to see the priest.

The woman judge granted the divorce on the fact that no matter how many decisions had to be made in the household, the husband always called round and asked the priest. And if the priest said no, then no it was.

What a story for the gutter press, it almost was – sex, marriage, cruelty, desertion, religion, litigation, generation gap and old-fashioned distemper. All it needed was a political angle.

The priest did have Russian connections. But because it was the Russian Orthodox Church and he himself was British to the core, not even the popular dailies could make much out of that:

'AGED RED MOLE PRIEST WRECKS BRITISH DIY MARRIAGE. God, Smithers, we give you a headline like that and you can't even make the facts fit? You're fired!'

An American being sued for divorce by his estranged wife decided to pre-empt any property settlement by cutting their home in half with a chain saw. When interviewed by the press, he'd already cut through the flooring of their single-storey house in Central City, Kentucky, and was taking a breather before getting a cutting torch to divide the bathtub.

His wife, who had moved out of the house a fortnight before, could not be reached for comment. Asked about her likely reaction, the husband – sounding not unduly distressed at the prospect – said: 'She might have a heart attack.'

He planned to carry on living in his half of the house. Presumably taking his baths elsewhere.

A divorced Yorkshireman, free of any wifely harassment, was able to carry on unhindered with the creation of the home of his dreams. He spent 10 years working on the three-bedroomed bungalow before dying of a heart attack.

Ten years' work should have left a little palace for the next occupants to move into. Not so. The house was such a mess that the estate agent halved the asking price. Dozens of projects had been left unfinished, and there was not a room in the place in which work already done did not need to be reversed.

Among the things which could have been done better was the demolition of inside brick walls and their replacement by fragile wooden supports. A door from a bedroom led into the garage. Another bedroom, described by the estate agent as 'the little black hole', had no windows or ventilation.

'He started one job and went on to the next without finishing it,' said the agent. 'The place looked as if it had been vandalised.'

'Ron was well-meaning,' said a neighbour. 'But things did not go right for him.'

Despite everything, the attractive half-price tag of £10,000 brought more than 100 prospective buyers to look round the place. And though the estate agent's sales pitch was hardly enthusiastic, there was one selling point which could not be denied – 'Suit do-it-yourself enthusiast.'

For nineteen years a British woman followed her airline pilot husband around the world, living in twenty-four different homes, always longing for a place they could really call their own.

They got it when the husband retired and bought a bargain house in Exmouth, Devon. But within two years, the wife told the Appeal Court, he had reduced the place to a shambles.

The judges were told that the husband moved thirty tons of rubble from under the house and dumped it in the garden; mixed cement in the living room; took off the toilet door and left it off for eight months. The floorboards he took up when they first moved in were still up two years later. Not only was the house cold, damp and draughty, the absence of a toilet door led to some embarrassment when visitors called.

At the original divorce court hearing, the judge had refused a decree on the grounds that a couple wed 'for better or worse'. But the three Appeal Court judges decided that the husband's 'unreasonable' behaviour really was unreasonable. Worse, as it were, than worse. Decree granted.

An amazing number of marriages, however, survive despite the efforts of the husband to improve the family home.

A housewife in Surrey went into the bedroom and disappeared through the floor. Her husband had taken up the floorboards and forgotten to tell her.

'I'd nipped round to the garage to fix the car,' he said. 'I want to do everything at once, that's my trouble.'

A business consultant in Richmond, Surrey, tried to replace the garden fence and drove a big wooden spike into the ground. He gave it an extra-heavy clout when it hit an obstruction, hammered it right through a main drain and flooded the garden.

Knocking his two garden sheds into one looked a much safer operation. But not long after he'd stepped back to admire his work, the back of the two-in-one shed fell off, the roof started leaking and the concrete base sank.

Retiling the kitchen floor was no problem until he ran out of purple tiles. The manufacturer had run out as well. So for a while the kitchen was tastefully tiled three-quarters purple and one-quarter white. The problem was finally solved by an attempt to re-plumb the dishwasher, which flooded the kitchen and lifted the tiles clean off. After the flood the kitchen door wouldn't shut, so off that came, propping up the wall until a professional could fit a new sliding door.

There was only one job remaining: sticking the wedding photographs in an album before the couple's Silver Wedding.

'A little job I've been meaning to get round to,' said the husband, 'for twenty-five years.'

Another Surrey handyman waved his wife off for the day and set to work putting in a sunken bath.

Eight hours later his wife returned to be greeted by plaintive cries for help. The husband had tried to lift the old bath, slipped, and spent the whole day trapped underneath.

This book, incidentally, is humbly and respectfully dedicated to a British journalist who would be nameless if he wasn't John Harvey. John, whose wife is very understanding, also lives in Surrey (what is it about the place that attracts 'em?) and he didn't have a lot of luck with God and his neighbour when he built an extension to his house.

During the excavations, John discovered an old well and decided to fill it in with bricks from a demolished chimney stack he just happened to have in his front room. It rained hard during the night – an Act of God, could happen to anybody – and the brick-filled well overflowed. The water flooded his next-door neighbour's kitchen.

Though conscious of the fact that his neighbour was not exactly over the moon about having to paddle to the kitchen sink, John decided to carry on with a project he was doing at the same time: digging a cesspit.

He'd got a nice big pit dug, all ready for the tank to be put in next day. But that night it rained hard – a freak storm, another Act of God. And his neighbour's lawn slid gently into the pit.

Relations by this time were not what could be described as cordial. (God was all right, but the neighbour was distinctly tetchy.) Nor were they improved when the neighbour rushed out and chopped down the garden hedge at the spot where John was preparing a barbecue for the kids.

But they reached the lowest point when John attempted to put the roof on his extension. The neighbour had claimed that John's eaves overhung the boundary. To emphasise his point he climbed onto the roof, ripped off the tiles, and threw them at John one by one.

'Funny chap,' said John. Just before he moved.

Another contender for the title of Mister Disaster Area is the London lift engineer whose skills seemed to desert him when he tackled anything at home.

Attempting to put up a new shower curtain, he fell from the ladder. The ladder cracked the bath panel, the flying drill smashed the wash basin and a hammer knocked a hole in the bath.

When he was removing a fireplace in the living room, a piece of concrete fell on his toe. As he jerked his battered foot free, the concrete flew off and went straight through the television screen.

The next project was painting the lavatory window, working outside from a ladder. The ladder slipped and he crashed through the roof of the car port below. A bricklayer's chisel he was using flew through the open window and cracked the lavatory bowl.

He forgot to warn his wife when he was working under the kitchen sink with an electric drill. His wife pulled the plug after washing some socks. Water from the disconnected waste pipe drenched the unfortunate husband and the drill. There was a flash, a bang, and the whole house was blacked out.

Then his wife bought some expensive Italian tiles for the kitchen and put them out of harm's way in the hall. On his way downstairs to start the laying job, the husband tripped, fell onto the tiles and smashed the lot.

Getting away from it all, he started to paint the front of the house. The paint pot, hanging from the ladder by a hook, tipped over – showering brilliant white paint onto his dark blue Cortina parked underneath.

Out rushed wifey to the rescue with a hose to wash down the car. It didn't get all the paint off, but it did dilute it enough to whitewash half the street.

The husband's last reported plan was to install a shower and wash basin in the bedroom. Any objections from his wife? (At the time she was recovering in hospital from an operation entirely unconnected with DIY).

'She is a patient lady,' he said.

CHAPTER THREE

It's a Promise

Do-it-yourself is now so much a part of the domestic scene that the traditional vows made at the altar don't begin to prepare a couple for the trials ahead.

As the vows stand, any husband can turn round and say, 'Nobody mentioned anything about plastering. I promised to love, comfort, honour and keep you, which seemed enough to be going on with. Where's there anything in the marriage service which says I have to slosh around in wet plaster, risking double pneumonia and putting my back out? Not to mention missing the pub?'

All this will change as the proposed new DIY marriage service gains currency. Though it retains the majesty of language of the old vows, and indeed contains promises much more awesome, it covers the realities of 20th-century marriage. Purely as a contract it is much more detailed and specific. So far, the World Council of Churches is rumoured to be less than enthusiastic about the vows, but they are believed to have the full blessing of the Builders Merchants Federation.

Here, then, is what the couple of the future will be promising each other:

The man is asked:
'Wilt thou have this woman to thy wedded wife, to live together in a state of constant material improvement, which is to say domestic turmoil and physical and mental exhaustion?

'Wilt thou at her behest hie forth in all weathers and return laden with all manner of woods, plastics, papers, fabrics and metals, knowing full well that thy beer money is gone for the month? Wilt thou return likewise with all manner of brushes, adhesives and tools, the purpose of which thou knowest but little, and about the operation of which thou hast not a clue?

'Wilt thou at her further behest hie thee up all manner of ladders and scaffoldings, risking limbs and thy very life, to attach such woods, plastics, papers, fabrics and metals with such adhesives, brushes and tools, to the furthest reaches of thy dwelling place?

'Before so doing, wilt thou promise to refrain from strong drink and noxious spirits, that thine eye may be true and thy hand be sure? That thou wilt neither skimp nor botch nor cock up the task appointed thee? And further that thou wilt not let thy foot stray from the perilous paths before thee, nor stumble nor slip so that thou comest crashing down from on high to damage the appurtenances of thy dwelling place, the appurtenances of thyself or thy beloved, or any onlooker below, thine ox or thine ass; yea, even thy dog, thy cat and thy budgie?

'Shouldst thou so descend from on high, wilt thou refrain from uttering loud oaths or imprecations, and from laying about thee to do harm to those who may find cause for mirth or merriment in thy misfortune?

'Wilt thou refrain from leaving thy dwelling place, calling down curses upon all thy works, and hieing thee to the inn, there to

indulge in strong drink and noxious spirits and to consort with publicans and sinners, whose ways are not the ways of the righteous do-it-yourselfer?

'Having so refrained, wilt thou then – should thy body be whole and not smitten hip and thigh – ascend again on high in cheerful heart to finish the task before thee and to repair the damage thou hast done?

'When at eventide thou has fulfilled the task appointed thee, wilt thou then take down from on high all the ladders and scaffoldings and bear them to a place of safekeeping? Wilt thou do likewise with thy brushes and tools, making them first clean and straight? Wilt thou dispose of all shards and gleanings and morsels of adhesives, woods, plastics, papers, fabrics and metals for which thou hast no further use? And wilt thou sweep up after thee?

'When all these tasks are done, will thou accept modestly and with an humble heart any praise which is bestowed on thee? For verily it is easier for a camel to pass through the eye of a needle than for a bighead to enter the Kingdom of Heaven. And should it be pointed out to thee that thou hast missed a bit in the highest corner of on high, wilt thou restrain thy tongue from cursing and thy hand from smiting, even to thy wedded wife, so long as ye both shall live – yea, even to thy wedded wife's mother?'

The woman is asked:

'Wilt thou have this man to thy wedded husband, to foster in him the arts of home improvement?

'Wilt thou prepare the path before him, so that his feeble excuses are but as sounding brass and tinkling cymbal?

'Wilt thou measure up, choose the colours, match the patterns, and order the materials, so that his way be made straight? For sloth's name is man, who canst think up more excuses than there are birds of the air or lilies of the field.

'Wilt thou then deflect his feet from the paths of unrighteousness? For verily, in the boozer temptation lies. Wilt thou let him not waste his substance in riotous living, nor pawn his power tools for a mess of pottage, and point him in the way of uprightness?

'Wilt thou counsel him wisely as he labours in the high places? Wilt thou make thy bearing meek and thy manner humble so as not to arouse his wrath, but still point out those things he has done which he ought not to have done, and those things he has not done which he ought to have done? For if the labourer is to be worthy of his hire, then should he neither skimp nor botch nor cock things up, nor should he work in haste to finish before the pubs shut.

'Wilt thou be also as his handmaiden, fetching and carrying as he bids thee, and pay no heed to the words of his mouth, yea, though hammers smite his thumbs and screwdrivers pierce his vitals?

'Wilt thou bind his wounds with sweet ointments and Elastoplast? Wilt thou kiss better his poorly finger, and with soft words soothe the raging in his breast?

'Wilt thou succour him with cool sherbets and cups of strong tea, and wilt thou keep up his strength with meats and breads and chips and fishes?

'Wilt thou also keep from him the temptation of strong drink until his task is finished and he is safely down from the high places?

'Wilt thou also keep from him those who may displease him as he labours, such as the fruit of thy loins who make mock of his travail while lifting nary a finger themselves? Wilt thou remove from his path thy dog, thy cat, thy budgie, yea, even thine hamster, who may cause him to stumble and fall; or who may be fallen upon, or painted by mischance like a coat of many colours? Above all things, wilt thou keep from his sight and his hearing thine own mother? She may be vexatious in his sight, causing him to wax wrath and fill the air with blaspheming.

'Wilt thou help him to dispose of the shards and gleanings and morsels when his labour is ended? Wilt thou soothe his fevered brow and whisper comforting words? Wilt thou then take the bottle of whisky from its hiding place and comfort him with strong drink?

'Wilt thou assure him of his mighty worth and of the excellence of the tasks he has completed? And wilt thou make no mention of the tasks to come, leaving it until he slumbers and sleeps before thou takest out the next book of wallpaper patterns, it being better for his repose that he wot not of what thou wist, nor even wist of what thou wot?'

CHAPTER FOUR

A Short History of Do-It-Yourself

The history of DIY starts with the Creation. God was the first DIY enthusiast, if only out of necessity. There was nobody around to help, let alone nag.

Given the time, He didn't do too badly, but today there are still complaints about how He handled His two trickiest jobs: creating man and woman. The complaints come mainly from male chauvinists in the form of sexist jokes, which none the less cannot be ignored by serious students of theology or DIY.

Some such jokes, or alleged jokes, as:

> God made Adam first because He didn't want any advice on how to do it.
>
> God made the first loudspeaker. Out of Adam's rib.
>
> God created the world and then He rested. Next He created man, and rested. Then He created woman. Since then, neither God nor man has rested.

Tut tut. But it's a measure of the strength and staying power of male chauvinism that Adam has ever since been given the credit for the first self-improvement projects. The image of Adam as pioneer has headed the list of those we are exhorted to look up to in matters of self-sufficiency, though at first he didn't have to do a thing for himself: in the Garden of Eden everything was laid on for him.

We have the evidence of the Good Book that Eve started it all with her ill-advised dietetic experiment. It caused her to look at

Adam in a new light and made him smarten himself up. Determined not to be outdone, Adam decided to do something himself and turned over a new leaf.

'Not mine, you fool,' said Eve. 'It's clean on.'

But by then it was too late.

The Americans took up the image of Adam as pioneer in a big way. As the *Cincinnati Bulletin* once thundered: 'Man was sent into this world to earn his living by the sweat of his brow. You didn't find Adam walking around the Garden of Eden with his hands in his pockets.'

And that's a fact.

To the Americans, self-sufficiency is what made their country what it is today. You've got to lay the blame somewhere. And certainly the men who built the West were a very special breed. As one American newspaper said of them: 'Our brave pioneers worked with an axe in one hand, a gun in the other, and a Bible in the other.'

Those men started young, too. As another newspaper proclaimed: 'Abraham Lincoln was born in a house which he helped his father to build.'

But the Americans can't claim all the credit: do-it-yourself is an ancient occupation and knows no frontiers of race or religion. There was the Quaker handyman, for instance, who opened the first do-it-thyself shop. And think of the martyrs of the movement, starting with Venus de Milo, who never could get the hang of carpentry. Either that or she bit her nails something chronic.

Then there was the Irish handyman who was caught up in the French Revolution and condemned to the guillotine. He knelt on the scaffold and the great blade fell – but halfway down it jammed. The executioner tried several times, but each time the blade jammed halfway down. He had decided to give up and allow the condemned man his freedom, when the Irishman looked up at the wedged blade and said, 'I see it now. Here's yer trouble. Just take out this nail here, and . . .'

All the great pioneers of history, in fact, have been do-it-yourselfers. They had to be: if a thing hasn't been done before, it's no use trying to get somebody else to do it.

Let's look at some of these great Firsts of History, and see what we owe to our DIY forefathers.

Stick It on the Wall

The great prehistoric cave paintings were the first attempts at wall covering.

Early Man was quite happy with the caves as they were, bare

walls and all. At least they were warm, dry, and a refuge from the dangers outside.

Then Early Woman got into the act.

'Are you going to sit around this cave all day doing nothing? Just look at those walls – nothing but stalactites and pterodactyl droppings! As soon as you've been out and got a couple of bison for dinner, you're going to roll up your loincloth [sleeves hadn't been invented] and get cracking!'

So the poor lad got cracking. And what happened?

As soon as he'd painted a few bison romping across the cave, the little woman didn't like them. Preferred a couple of mammoths. When she got the mammoths, she thought that a flight of dodos would be more tasteful [dodos hadn't yet learned *not* to fly]. She wanted dodos, she got dodos. And then she changed her mind again.

'Why not a few hairy rhinoceroses, like Missis Piltdown next-cave? Her Ug has done some very tasteful hairy rhinoceroses. And you should see his elks . . .'

Muttering, 'Sod Ug. *And* his elks,' poor old Early Man got cracking again. There was a limit to the wall space in all but the biggest caves, and finally he was reduced to painting one scene on top of another, which is why the average prehistoric mural looks such a mess.

The art of cave painting came to an abrupt end somewhere in the middle of the New Stone Age. One theory has it that the new stone was much easier to swing in a cave than the old stuff. And that Early Woman eventually learned to keep quiet. If she didn't want a flat head.

Keeping Mum

The Great Pyramid near Giza in Egypt, one of the Seven Wonders of the World, was built during the 2600s BC by the Pharaoh Khufu. (*Gesundheit*.)

He intended the massive structure as a tomb for his mother-in-law: not so much to honour her passing as to make sure she couldn't get out. It was originally designed as a cube.

There are many theories about the evolution from cube to pyramid, including:

1 An aggrieved householder in Cairo putting up an *Ancient Egyptian Lights* notice.

2 The use of Irish bricklayers, who were the only ones who could carry up the bricks, even if they didn't know a cube when they saw one.

3 The use of bricklayers from the hills, who traditionally had one leg shorter than the other and tended to build in ever-decreasing circles.

4 An unforeseen shortage of bricks, overcome in later years by getting the Israelites to make them without straw. But at this time there was an unforeseen shortage of Israelites. 'They're never around when you need 'em,' said Khufu. (*Gesundheit.*)

The most likely explanation, however, is the appearance from the east of a wandering hermit, who brought with him the new science of accountancy.

The hermit was brought before Khufu (Oh, forget it), complaining that he had stubbed his toe on a pile of bricks in the desert.

'Pile of bricks, nothing,' said Khufu. 'That's the beginning of my giant cube.'

'Cube, shmube,' said the hermit. 'For why are you wanting such a cube?'

The Pharaoh explained.

'Oy, oy,' said the hermit. 'Such a cube for one little babushka! Make it hollow! That way you save 90 per cent. Less, of course, a small commission.'

'No way,' said Khufu. 'When that old bat goes down, she stays down.'

'OK,' said the hermit. 'Tell you what. Instead of a cube, you have a pyramid. Stick babushka in dead centre of base, and any way she moves, she got trouble. *You* got no more trouble and you save 50 per cent. Less, of course, a small commission.'

'I like it, I like it!' exclaimed Khufu. 'It's a deal. You know, of course, that I could make you a slave, but for this idea I'll make you a freedman. What's your name, by the way?'

'Milton,' said the hermit. 'And how do you spell that freedman . . . ?'

(End of feeble monetarism joke.)

There is little more to tell about the Great Pyramid, except that it was built and stands to this day, towering 450 feet – less, of course, a small commission – over the sands. And that one day there was the inevitable sad homecoming for Khufu's wife.

'Yoo-hoo!' she called, dropping her shopping and approaching her mother's chambers. 'Mother! I'm home!'

There was no reply. The chambers were empty, though with signs of a hasty departure. After searching the whole palace in vain, she burst into Khufu's study.

'Khufu!' she cried. 'I want my mother! Where's my mother?'

Khufu gave a wry smile and gazed out of the window towards the massive Pyramid.

'You'll find her over there, my love,' he said, sweetly. 'Turn left past the Sphinx and first on your . . .'

'You mean the Pyramid?' exclaimed Khufu's wife. 'That's nice. She's always taken a great interest in that.'

'So she has,' said Khufu. 'In fact you could say now that she's really wrapped up in it. And though she may have been a mother to you, from now on she'll always be a mummy to me . . .'

The Unkindest Cut

Samson, hero of ancient Israel, had the strength of ten men and did much more work about the house than any of his neighbours, the Philistines. Not only were they jealous of the amount of work he got through, they were also very peeved when he accidentally killed 1,000 of them with the jawbone of an ass he was using to trim the hedge.

'Serve 'em right,' said Samson. 'They shouldn't have been lurking about there in the first place. Bloody rubbernecks.'

The Philistines were determined to get their revenge, and they learned that the secret of Samson's strength lay in his hair. So they started a whispering campaign, aimed at Samson's girlfriend, Delilah.

'He really is a hard grafter,' they said. 'And it's all very well when he's doing jobs inside the house. But when he works outside, he lowers the tone of the whole neighbourhood. That hair! What a scruff! Property values are plummeting. Of course, it's none of our business, but if we were you, girl, we'd get him tidied up a bit.'

Samson refused. He was proud of his flowing locks and would let nobody touch them. So one day, when he was sleeping it off after a well-earned session at the *Gaza Arms*, Delilah did a do-it-yourself job on his hair. It has since stood as an awful warning to anybody trying a home perm for the first time.

When Samson woke up he was furious. There he was, as weak as a kitten – and the world's first skinhead, to boot.

The Philistines captured him, booted him, and started to ridicule his DIY skills.

'How do you make a Phoenician blind?' they asked.

'Well,' replied Samson, 'you get some wooden slats and you – '

'Wrong!' cried the Philistines. 'You do this – .' And laughingly poked his eyes out.

They made him work as a slave on a job training scheme for a while, then took him to their temple to boast about the new extension they'd put up. In their glee they didn't notice that his hair had grown again.

'Just feel that brickwork,' they said, leading him to the pillars supporting the temple. 'They don't lay 'em like that any more, eh?'

Samson felt around the pillars and poked his finger into the substandard mortar the Philistines had used.

'Load of rubbish,' he said. 'Why, one good shove and the whole lot would – whoops!'

. . . And so, as any good chiropodist will tell you, Samson became the first man in the world to die from fallen arches.

Unfinished Business

Stonehenge is a splendid example of Ancient British DIY, or Druid-Yourself, as it was known then. It was intended as an indoor barbecue hall, roast prisoner being an Ancient British delicacy at the summer solstice. It took several hundred years to build, mainly because of the size of the stones and the fact that some of them had to be carted 200 miles from western Wales. (A Support-Local-Industries campaign in Wiltshire failed to have any effect, possibly because the Druids in charge of the building work were major shareholders in the Welsh quarries.)

There was a high incidence of bad backs among the hod carriers because the stones weighed an average of twenty-eight tons, a fact which was alluded to on the tombstone of one of them, an Irish guest worker by the sound of it:

Here lies Paddy,
Crossed the Styx.
He'd be here now
If they'd thought of bryx.

Time for the topping-out ceremony came round about 4,000 years ago.

'Right, boyos,' intoned the Archdruid, waving his holy leek, 'we're nearly there. A few trips to Prescelly for another thirty bluestones and there is your roof, isn't it? If we all pull together for another few hundred years, we can relax and enjoy ourselves. There's beer on the house, look you, and as many people as you can eat. What do you say?'

The unfortunate Archdruid was standing in front of a 16-foot

upright block of sandstone which marked the centre of the barbecue pit. In the rush for the free beer, the stone was toppled and he was flattened. When the barbecue was over and the beer ran out, everybody went home.

To this day, the large stone lies flat in the centre of Stonehenge, and nobody's bothered to finish the roof. Not so much because the work force totally lost interest, but because the Archdruid had the plans in his pocket.

There is no woman in this story. Which is why it is a classic example of well being left alone. If the Archdruid had been rescued, which would have seemed the sensible thing to do and which a woman would certainly have thought of, Stonehenge might now be just on the verge of completion. And a county planning inspector might be on the verge of having it pulled down. There's no damp course, for a start . . .

The Height of Ambition

Nebuchadnezzar II was the King of Babylon from 605 to 562 BC. Though in his prime he was a terrible man for the conquering and laying waste, he rarely mentioned it in later years, preferring to write about his many building projects. He had other forms of madness as well, such as going out into the fields on all fours and eating grass.

'Why don't you stop him?' asked the high priests of his wife.

'I would,' she said, 'but we need the milk.'

His wife was a princess from the mountains, and she grew sad living in the flat lands of Babylonia. 'They're so – what's the word? – *plain*,' she said.

'I know,' said Nebby, spitting out a mouthful of grass. 'That's why I like 'em.'

Then he burst into song:

> Ba-ha-ha-ha-haa-bee-lonia!
> Where the wind comes sweeping down the plain!
> And the corn smells sweet
> Under my four feet
> And the –

'Oh, shut up and finish your fodder,' said his wife. 'You've got to admit that this place needs a certain something. A mountain or two, perhaps.'

'Leave it to me,' said Nebby, and quick as a flash drew up the plans for the Hanging Gardens.

For many long years, armies of labourers toiled, and armies of toilers laboured, to build a huge sweep of terraces that seemed to soar to the sky.

The garden's as high
As an elephant's eye –

sang Nebby.

'Oh, shut up,' said his wife.

When the building work was finished, the terraces were filled with the best soil in the land and planted with the finest, most colourful and scented flowers, shrubs and trees, a process which took many more long years.

At last, all was ready, and Nebuchadnezzar took his princess to view the Gardens in full bloom. The sight dazzled the eyes. The perfume intoxicated the senses. The sheer mass of the project – four acres supported on pillars and rising in terraces for 300 feet in the air – dwarfed everything around it. Not since the Pyramids had there been such a spectacle.

'I did it all for you, my love,' said the proud king. 'How's that for the second Wonder of the World? The Hanging Gardens of Babylon. Not bad, eh?'

'Very nice,' said the princess, unenthusiastically. Then, noticing Nebuchadnezzar's downcast expression, she said hastily, 'No, truly, Nebby love. They're really very beautiful. But I think I would have preferred them over *there* . . .'

Colour It Blue

The Ancient Britons were great painters, but the Roman emperor Claudius found the whole scene pretty dreary. Everything in Britain was painted blue with the traditional woad.

When the great British chief Caractacus was hauled before him in chains, Claudius asked, 'Why blue? Everywhere I look, nothing but blue?'

'It's a beautiful colour,' said Caractacus. 'It's the colour of the sky on a fine summer day, the colour of a calm sea, the colour of the bluebird as she flits from bough to bough, the colour of the eyes of a beautiful maiden, the colour of the woodland flowers as they unfold their delicate petals in the spring.'

'Even so,' said Claudius, 'don't you find it a bit monotonous?'

'Boring as hell,' said Caractacus. 'But it's the only colour we've got.'

There are many accounts of the Ancient Britons charging into battle painted blue from top to toe, frightening the life out of the Roman legions. Claudius was curious about this, too. Did the application of woad give the warriors a fanatical urge to fight?, he asked. Did it fill them with some superhuman power?

'You must remember,' said Caractacus, 'that these lads aren't full-time soldiers. When they got their call-up papers they were all busy painting their humble abodes. So far nobody's come up with a non-drip woad – and you just can't get the stuff off.'

'But what about their battle frenzy?' persisted Claudius. 'Why does the woad turn them into raging furies? What causes them to rush about so?'

'You ever tried that woad?' asked Caractacus. 'Talk about *itch* . . .'

Another thing that impressed Claudius was the intricacy of the

patterns the Ancient Britons painted: a mad Celtic whirl of curves, circles and spirals. Hardly a straight line anywhere. 'Why?' he asked.

'Traditional,' said Caractacus. 'We have an Ancient British saying: "It's a long woad that has no turning".'

. . . There is a woman in the case, as there is in most significant events in DIY history. When he was fleeing from the Romans, Caractacus took refuge with Cartimandua, Queen of the Brigantes, a northern tribe. It was she who gave him up to Claudius. Legend has it that she was fed up with him wandering round her kingdom, painting everything blue.

Feeling Down . . .

One of the most important influences on any DIY operation is gravity. This is the force which causes unattached objects to move towards the centre of the Earth until they are stopped by the Earth's surface or some other intervening body.

Gravity was discovered in 1687 by the intervening body of the English scientist Isaac Newton. An apple fell on his head as he took tea in the garden, causing him to utter the immortal words which have resounded down the centuries: 'Ouch!' as the apple landed, and 'Aaaargh!' as the scalding tea went all down his trousers.

He staggered indoors to find his old mother kneeling on the ceiling with a paint brush in one hand and a pot of paint in the other.

'Hello, Ikey, my love,' she said, cheerfully wielding the brush. 'My, my, just look at the state of you. What have you been up to now, you young rascal?'

'Mother!' cried Isaac, horrified. 'You shouldn't be kneeling on the ceiling like that! Don't you know it's against the laws of gravity?'

With an almighty crash, his mother fell to the floor. Covered in paint and bruises, she looked up at him angrily.

'You and your big mouth!' she cried. 'Another five minutes and I'd have finished!'

After a short session in intensive care, Newton and his mother were fit to face the world again: she to finish the ceiling standing on a ladder, he to announce his findings to the Royal Society.

The Fellows of the Royal Society were disbelieving when Newton first outlined his discovery.

'Prove it!' they cried.

'Look at this!' shouted Isaac above the barracking, whipping off his wig to disclose a large lump on his head. 'And that was only from the apple. The tea did far more damage – you should see my poor intervening body!'

'Go on, then!' cried the Fellows.

Leaping onto a chair, Isaac dropped his trousers, but this only brought further screams of disbelief from the Fellows, mixed with bursts of hysterical laughter and the odd dog latin tag, or latin dog tag, such as 'Parvum in multo!' and 'Ecce pecky!'

Beside himself with rage, Isaac stepped from the chair, tripped on his trousers and fell flat on his podium, which splintered beyond repair.

This finally convinced the Fellows that what goes up must come down, though they insisted that Newton add a rider to the effect that, in the case of trousers, what comes down ought to go back up if one is not to keep falling flat on one's podium.

Recognition finally came to Newton in 1705 when he was knighted by Queen Anne. At the time she was not yet dead, but she was getting a bit shaky on her pins.

'Watch what you're doing with that sword, woman,' muttered the kneeling Newton, crusty old bachelor that he was, and mindful that the good Queen had inadvertently beheaded 25 per cent of all recent prospective knights.

News of Newton's discovery had further drastic effects as it filtered through to the outside world. It set back the burgeoning DIY craze for years, as home handymen came crashing to the ground in their thousands.

Severe subsidence hit the great Wall of China, the Hanging Gardens of Babylon fell down, the Tower of Pisa leaned dangerously, Atlantis sank and the Colossus of Rhodes ruptured himself. The Pyramids, thanks to their shape, stayed upright. But the last riddle asked of the Sphinx – 'What's up when it's raining and down when it's fine?* – caused it to have a sneezing fit and its nose fell off. The Sphinx's last recorded words were, 'I thuppothe you thig thad's bluddy fuddy.' And after that there was silence.

Newton, mind you, was not the first to study gravity. Galileo, in 1590, had experimented with falling bodies by dropping cannonballs and bricks from the Leaning Tower of Pisa. Whatever the size of the cannonballs or bricks, they tended to hit the ground at the same time, unless stopped by an intervening body such as that of a passing peasant. Though this did not lead to any conclusions about gravity, it did help to alleviate the problems of over-population among passing peasantry.

Michelangelo could have got away with painting the Sistine Chapel ceiling without scaffolding, working as he did (1505–12) before Galileo had even begun to drop bricks. But his scientific research had suggested that such a thing as gravity might exist and would one day be proven.

'I just don't want to be up there when it happens,' said Mike. 'Not without visible means of support.'

. . . Why, you may ask, were the laws of gravity not discovered in the Third World? Why not in one of the great civilisations that existed in ancient times, when we in the West were still naked savages?

The answer is not far to seek. Fruit in warmer climes is heavier and more abundant. Anyone struck while sitting under a coconut or breadfruit tree seldom lived to tell the tale. Not only is the fruit heavier but the trees are taller, so the fruit has farther to fall. A falling body drops 16 feet in the first second, and thereafter accelerates by 32 feet per second.

Newton was probably struck by a moderately sized apple travelling at only 16 feet per second. Third World philosophers would have been struck by large coconuts, or bunches of large coconuts, travelling at up to 80 feet per second. This would cause

* Answer: an umbrella. With which the Sphinx was not familiar, the Egyptian climate being what it was.

them to lose their train of thought, if not their whole interest in the subject. If asked about gravity as they were carted off from under the tree, their comment, roughly translated from the Sanskrit, would be: 'Gravity? Oh, *sod* gravity . . .'

Victorian Values

It is a little-known fact that the poet Rudyard Kipling took his pen name from an encounter with a craftsman working at his mother's home.

The young Kipling – his real name was William Shakespeare, and his agent had told him he'd never get anywhere with a name like that – had wracked his brains for months, trying to think up a new name. One day he was wandering absentmindedly through the corridors when he fell over a bucket filled with plaster.

'Fancy leaving that where I could fall over it, you oaf!' roared Master Shakespeare. 'I'll get mama to have you flogged within an inch of your life! Or better still, transported!'

(You could talk to people like that in those days. Victorian manners towards the lower orders were shocking.)

'Oh, young Master Shakespeare, sir, please do not tell your mama of my stupidity and ineptitude!' beseeched the workman. 'I have a wife and 11 children, all relying on me to bring home a few morsels to keep body and soul together. My Tiny Tim is suffering from a ricket – we can afford but the one – and if I lose my employment he will surely die!

'So have pity, young sir! Spare a humble and poverty-stricken artisan! Have a thought for his humble and poverty-stricken wife and humble and poverty-stricken children! And if these sentiments do not move you, young sir – I'll knock your bleedin' 'ead orf . . .'

So moved was the young man that he immediately forgave the honest artisan and took an interest in his work.

'What were you doing with that plaster, pray?' he asked.

'Kipplin', young sir. I was a-kipplin' of this 'ere wall. Very skilled work it is. A dyin' trade as you might say. Not much call for it these days.'

'It looks easy enough to me.'

'Don't let that deceive you, sir,' said the artisan. 'It's nowhere near as easy as it looks. In fact, if you'll pardon the expression, it's ruddy 'ard.'

'I've got it!' cried the youth.

'Well don't come near me!' cried the workman. 'I've got enough trouble as it is!'

'No, you fool – my new name. Ruddyard Kippling! Here, take

this farthing and buy Tiny Tim all the rickets he can eat . . .'

And so the great poet began his career under a name that has since resounded around the world, at least in its modified form.

His first poems were typeset in Hong Kong to take advantage of the cheaper DIY rates there. The cost-cutting Cantonese-speaking typesetters were unaware of the importance of double consonants, and the name came back on proof as Rudyard Kipling.

'Leave it as it is,' said his publisher. 'Corrections cost money. And I'm not forking out another bowl of rice for anybody. Who the hell's to know, anyway?'

Apart from providing him with a name, the encounter with the artisan gave young Kipling a deep and abiding interest in do-it-yourself, as can be seen from an early version of what later, after a few alterations, became one of his most famous poems:

If you can keep your tools when all about you
    Are losing theirs and blaming it on you,
If you can sweep the chimney single-handed
    And not leave the head of the brush stuck up the flue;
If you can plug the walls to take the bookshelves
    And not have the lot collapse around your ears,
Or being nagged at, don't give way to cursing,
    And yet don't raid the fridge for all those beers.

If you can put the paper on the ceiling
    And not have it peel back off before it's dry,
If neither foes nor know-all friends can peeve you
    And you don't get bits of plaster in your eye;
If you can fill the unforgiving bucket
    With spade after spade of concrete, three-to-one;
Get down to the pub before it's time to chuck it.
    Forget the work and just get smashed, my son!

CHAPTER FIVE

Kitted Out

A way of easing yourself into DIY, taking the fiddling detail out of a job, or just cutting out some of the hard work, is to buy a kit.

You can buy kits for almost anything, from earrings to sea-going boats. A cardboard box manufacturer in Sheffield is even producing cardboard coffins in kit form for assembly at home. Certainly the coffins do cut funeral costs drastically. It could be a bit of a shock for an indisposed DIY man, though, when his wife hands him the easy-assembly kit she's bought to help pass the time. ('I thought you'd like this, dear. Only £25. Well, you're so much better at this kind of thing than I am. And I thought there's no point in *waiting* . . .')

Orders for coffins, of course, are dealt with straightaway, but most manufacturers' advertisements for DIY kits give an approximate delivery date. So if you read 'Allow 14 days for delivery', you know that it will be on your doorstep in six weeks or so. Providing there's not an R in the month or a weekend in between.

Oh, the excitement when you hear that ring at the doorbell and the sound of feet runing back up the path. The running feet are those of the postman or delivery man who has just noticed that the parcel he has been slinging about all morning, and kicking out of the way in the back of the van, is marked FRAGILE: THIS SIDE UP.

Should the delivery man still be around when you open the door, he's likely to be convulsed with pain – having just ruptured himself carrying your Little Wonder Build-Your-Own-Battleship Kit – and either expecting a heavy tip or asking whom he should sue.

Make the most of your kit while it's still outside by letting the neighbours know all about it. 'Ah, darling! It's arrived. My Young Millionaire's Make-Your-Own-Crown-Jewels Kit. How absolutely spiffing!' Then take it indoors before they get a chance to read the label which announces that you're in receipt of the Senior Pauper's Build-It-Yourself Toothpaste-Tube-Squeezer.

Not that the neighbours need much warning of a special delivery. Often they know about it before you do. The classic example is of the delivery man who rang the doorbell to be answered by a voice shouting, 'Who is it?'

'A parcel for Mr Higginson,' he replied.

'Is it in a cardboard box, brown paper, or is it gift-wrapped?'

'Brown paper.'

'Where's it from?'

'Says here, "Charlie's Komprehensive Kit Emporium, Bradford".'

'What's in it?'

'I don't know for sure. Feels like some lengths of wood, sheets of hardboard, metal strips and packets of screws.'

'Well, couldn't you just open it and see?'

'Against regulations, tampering with parcels. Anyway, you'll find out for yourself if you'll just open the door and sign for it.'

'I can't sign for it.'

'Why not?'

'Because I'm not Mr Higginson. He lives next door.'

Before you send off for a kit, read the ad carefully. Often the claims are a bit lavish, if not confused:

> Give your home that fashionable Restoration look with this genuine reproduction Elizabethan four-poster bed – as slept in by Bluff King Hal! – complete with original Georgian tapestries and stylish Regency canopy!

And sometimes they tend towards the over-optimistic:

> Put up this splendid bed in a single evening! Easy assembly – so simple that even a child could do it!

It's only when you're struggling to fit Part Four to Part Five at three in the morning that you realise what the manufacturers meant: that the evening was based on winter in north Alaska, where the nights are six months long, and that the child referred to won the Nobel Prize for Maths and Physics (Junior Section) and was an Olympic gymnast to boot.

It pays to read the small print carefully, too. 'No saws, planes, drills, screws, nuts or bolts,' could mean just that. You may need 'em, but you don't get 'em.

> Don't wait for the deluge! Build your own full-size ark!
> Fabulous kit of materials as used by Noah himself!

For that you could get a few thousand cubits of gopher wood* and some buckets of pitch.

* Don't be surprised if the gopher wood bears an uncanny resemblance to common-or garden pine. It can mean almost anything: pine, fir, cedar, boxwood, turpentine tree, Indian plane tree, or cypress. Scholars have still not agreed on what wood Noah had to hand.

It is agreed, however, that the name caused a row between Noah and one of his sons. Noah was working on top of the ark when his son appeared below.

'Anything you want, Dad?' he called.

'Yes,' said Noah. 'Gopher wood.'

'But Dad . . . I'm getting fed up of –'

'Do as you're told. Gopher wood!'

'Isn't there anything else I can do, Dad? I've bin fer wood twice already!'

You've taken your kit indoors and have unwrapped it with trembling hands. (If it's a Home Brain Surgery Kit, wait until the trembling has subsided before you proceed.) The very first thing you must do now is read the instructions. Instructions are of several kinds:

1 Those which were mixed up with the wrappings, which you have taken outside and, in the interest of tidiness, order and method, incinerated.

2 Those which you shredded into lots of tiny pieces as you feverishly ripped off the wrappings. Trying to piece them back together makes for hours of jolly fun.

3 Those which the cat has run off with, the dog has eaten, or the kids are using outside as paper darts.

4 Those which are in separate sheet form. Very detailed and comprehensive. Or they would be if they didn't include four copies of Sheet One and no copies of Sheets Three, Four and Five.

5 A folded sheet with three or four pages printed on each side. Very handy for reference, unless they were prepared in the Far East. In which case, even though the English translation may be impeccable, you may find it advisable to start with the right-hand page and read back to the left.

6 Those translated abroad, using the services of a cut-price translator who had the additional handicap of not knowing the slightest thing about DIY. For example:

> Take up the spike in the left manual extremity and place the pointing of it at place A. Now be taking up the smiting tool in the right manual extremity, and with it applying concussion to the cranium of the spike. Concuss the cranium until it rests on the same plane as the surface of the tree, taking much care at all times to avoid trauma to the digits of the left manual extremity.

By the time you've worked out that you are placing the nail at point A and are hammering it level with the surface of the wood, the evening is half over. Not only that, in your impatience you forget the safety instruction and inflict severe digital trauma by bashing your left thumb.

7 Those written in English by native English speakers. Great. Now we're getting somewhere. Except that (a) they're incredibly pompous, (b) they overlook the fact that the average home handyman does not have a degree in engineering or a diploma in plumbing, and (c) he is not overly familiar with the technical terms used in that particular kit factory:

> Drill at a tangent through the plangent to facilitate the

attachment of the oscillating face-fixers, which should be firmly secured with domical-headed clanger clasps before connecting the galvanised gunge gurgler pipe by the corrugated bush projection of the reverse-slurping rubber insert cone.

Pardon?

8 Those in which the diagrams:

(a) Look like the plans for the wiring circuit of a space probe.

(b) Have been taken straight from the wall of a kindergarten art exhibition.

(c) Are non-existent. (This is sometimes an advantage. If the end result looks like nothing on earth, who's to criticise when there's nothing to compare it with?)

The choice of room for assembling your kit is very important. There is seldom room in the average shed, unless all you are into is cuckoo clocks. Kits laid out on the garage floor tend not to survive the arrival of whichever member of the family has borrowed the car. ('Dad! Who left those nails and bits of wood all over the garage floor? They've made a hell of a mess of the tyres!')

Working in the kitchen is cramped and obviously unlikely to be popular. But even should your presence be tolerated, it is difficult to fit part 232a to 232b in an ordinary oven. Or to work with hot spaghetti all over your head and meat sauce down the back of your neck.

Anyway, there you are with all the bits spread out on the floor, plans in hand and ready to start.

Before you so much as pick up a piece, check that everything's there. It's annoying to work for days on a scale model of Nelson's Column, and then find there's no Nelson. (Even more annoying to ring up the firm and be told: 'You bought our Nelson's *Column*, right? Did we say anything about *Nelson*?'

And check that you've got the plans the right way up. One keen but cack-handed amateur sent for a mail-order summer house kit. A few weeks later he wrote a letter of complaint to the manufacturer.

An inspector from the firm soon diagnosed the trouble. 'You've built the whole thing upside down,' he said.

'Oh, so *that's* it?' said the handyman. 'No wonder I kept falling off the porch.'

Be very careful that you use the bits and pieces for their proper purposes. If a piece doesn't fit, it doesn't necessarily mean shoddy workmanship at the factory. There may be another reason for it, such as its being the wrong bit. (The author has a hardwood garden bench-and-table set with the legs permanently bolted the wrong way to prove it.) So don't just bash it into submission or saw a bit off the end. When you come to fix the last piece of all, you'll probably find that it is short by precisely the same length as the other bit, now sawn down, was long.

It's the same with nuts, bolts, nails and screws. If one looks too long, check before you use it. At the next stage you'll be trying to fix sections with screws that are far too short and won't stretch. There aren't any spares in the packets and the shops are shut. Pity, when it's a replacement bay window and you've already taken the old one out.

Take care with any paints, adhesives or solvents supplied, and make sure they're mixed and applied precisely as instructed. Take warning from the impatient enthusiast who, without looking, squeezed what he thought was his yellow base paint into the thinner. When he used it, it came out a horrible colour and was full of bits of fluff. Just then his wife walked in, announcing, 'Look what I've found in the kitchen,' and handed him a tube of concentrated yellow.

'Bloody hell,' he said. 'I've just painted the bedpost with the canary.'

CHAPTER SIX

Mind How You — Whoops!

The past thirty years have seen the growth of DIY from small beginnings to a multi-billion pound international industry. The past fifteen years have seen a massive boom in sales – and a massive boom in home accidents.

A doctor writing in the *British Clinical Journal* of 1974 was among the first to warn about the Battered Husband Syndrome. The husbands he was mainly worried about were those who, after

spending their working weeks in sedentary office jobs, launched into 'wild uncharted seas of manual labour and Active Pursuits' at weekends.

'The unskilled in perilous pursuit of the unusable,' was how he described the activities of the gallant but cack-handed lads. Not only was the injury rate alarming; the nature of the injuries was horrifying. Hammers, axes, chisels, saws, drills and knives were taking a terrible toll. And that was before anybody had fallen off anything.

Cracked ribs, broken limbs, cut shins, aches, pains and strains were among the less gruesome of the afflictions. A feature of many of the accidents was their bizarre nature. At least hospital casualty staff got a laugh or two as they recorded the details. Among the star turns was the loony who tried to paint a wall while standing on a tea trolley: if his head wasn't cracked before, it certainly was afterwards.

Even should the DIY man be lucky enough to avoid actually piercing his vitals, breaking something, falling off something or setting fire to himself, his under-exercised muscles cannot cope with the sudden strain at weekends. Strain of the lumbar region, painter's wrist and soreness of the tendons are common. Not to mention the stomach upsets, headaches and nausea brought on by paint, solvent and adhesive fumes.

A recent British survey reckoned that in any given year, one in three home handymen takes time off work, or is subject to illnesses and injury to some degree, as a direct result of misdirected DIY activities. At the lowest estimate, the number of enthusiasts and dabblers in Britain alone adds up to more than 3,000,000. Higher estimates say a staggering 5,000,000. Which adds up to a lot of dicky do-it-yourselfers, even if the bulk of the injuries require only sticking plaster and kiss-it-better treatment.

'How can we avoid it?' you may well ask. It's not easy, but you must force yourself. Fight off all temptation to pick up a paintbrush, a chisel, a trowel or a drill. Keep both feet firmly on the ground, however much you long to clamber up ladders and scaffolding. Lift nothing heavier than a pint glass. And leave the tops on all containers of paint and other noxious substances.

It will be hard at first, with nothing to do during the long summer afternoons but lie in the garden, breaking the monotony only by listening to the grass grow and raising a glass of refreshing liquid to your parched lips. Nothing to do during the long winter evenings but lie on the settee, watching dreary football matches or boring old *Emmanuelle* videos, perhaps taking yourself off to the pub now and again out of consideration for your Nearest and Dearest, who is bound to be distressed by the sight of your DIY withdrawal symptoms.

Cold turkey of any kind is never a pleasant experience, but with fortitude and resolution you will in time overcome the craving to do something about the house, and will settle down to becoming a solid, safe, respectable and useless citizen.

It's the future you have to think of. What sort of future would you have with bits missing? How could you explain to your children that the shattered wreck they see before them, hardly recognisable as human, brought his condition upon himself by his insane lust for home improvement?

Remember that the future starts here. Starts now. So be strong. And in years to come you will still be sitting in front of the telly, sound in mind and limb, listening to the heartwarming bustle of family life. As the children rush around, repositioning buckets to catch the water running in from the caved-in roof; as your wife laughs gaily at the sound of plaster falling from the walls; as the wind whistles merrily through the broken window panes; as the dog disappears happily from sight through the dry rot in the floorboards; as the budgie coughs cheerily in the smoke from the blocked-up

chimney, you will rest content in the knowledge that your sacrifice was not in vain.

And as the family gazes lovingly at your recumbent form, which even in the autumn of your years lacks none of the bits you were born with, they will be able to say: 'Dear Papa. He did it all for us.'

Some Interesting Ways of Doing Yourself a Mischief

The ultimate technique for avoiding DIY is to be rendered unfit for it: to join the thousands of crocks groaning away in casualty wards, intensive care units, or in the privacy of their own homes, temporarily unable to bash in a nail, bore a hole in a wall or wheel a barrow. Or to join, on a more permanent basis, the happy band in the Great Discount Centre in the Sky, who arrived there after a spectacular bang, conflagration, self-impalement or 30-foot nose-dive.

All it needs is for you to do things your way: to hell with the safety instructions. What do these people think you are, anyway? Some sort of incompetent?

You know what you're doing. You're perfectly fit for the job. You were doing it before half these whingeing, interfering know-it-alls were potty trained. To hell with them and their namby-pamby approach. Let's get on with it your own way . . .

Ladders? What, for a simple job like this? No, the dustbin will do fine. Need to stretch over a bit to reach that far corner, but what the hell.

OK, so you do need ladders for that guttering job. Shove 'em tight to the wall, that's the answer. All that rubbish about one foot out to four feet up. You'd never get the height if you did that. And stake them at the bottom and lash them at the top? Give over. Take all day fiddling about.

The rungs? Nothing wrong with the rungs. They've stood up well for 30 years, rain or shine, those rungs. As sound as the day you first set foot on them.

Careful carrying the ladders round that corner? Why? Nobody's coming. What? Well, that's his flaming fault for not looking where he was going. Pick him up, somebody.

Aluminium ladders, they're the thing. Light as a feather. One quick shove and they're 30 feet up in the – *what* power cable?

Chisels? Plenty of chisels somewhere in that old biscuit tin with the screwdrivers and odd bits of wire. On that bottom shelf, near where the kids are playing.

Of course the chisels aren't masked: never have been. You can put your hand on the one for the job just like that. Some old razor blades in the bottom of the tin, too, for the smaller jobs.

While you're at it, let's have that old craft knife to trim the edge of this carpet. Bit rusty, but what do you expect? Still plenty good enough. Gloves? No need to bother with gloves for a one-off job like this.

Gloves for glass? Why? Nothing to it if you know what you're doing. And there's no need to replace those cracked panes in the top of the greenhouse. They're good for years yet. Whoops! Just pick the bits out of your neck and throw them onto the lawn. The kids will find them sooner or later.

Didn't take long to finish the patio and the garden path. So what if one or two slabs are sticking up? You know where they are. All you have to do is pick your feet up and go carefully in the dark.

Instant contact adhesives never bond as quickly as they're supposed to. Only one way to tell if it's touch-dry: give it a quick prod.

Right, we'll soon clear this loft. Planks across the joists? What for? Just step from joist to joist. You're not crippled, for God's sake. (Not yet.)

A bit of drilling now. Marvellous things, these power tools. Just plug it into that adaptor. There are two power plugs in already? It takes three, doesn't it? Of course the wire's all right. That break was mended only this morning. Perfectly good insulating tape, that. Or is it the black plastic stuff?

No room for two down there to lift that thing out. Nor for any of that nonsense about knees bent, feet slightly apart, grip firm and back straight. No, the only way to shift this is to bend over it, get the finger tips under the edge and – aargh!

Nothing like the old blowlamp for quick results. Quicker if you don't turn it off in between using it. If it runs out of fuel, don't bother waiting for it to cool down. Just bung in some more. And pump it up hard: you want to burn the stuff off, not lightly poach it.

Don't bother having a bucket of water or fire extinguisher handy: only something else to clutter up the place. And don't waste time clearing all that straw and old birds' nests from under the eaves: one quick blast from the old lamp will take care of that lot.

As soon as you've finished, get yourself down to the pub. You can't hang about for an hour to check whether anything's smouldering. Never is, when you're watching it.

Let's get this grass cut before the pubs shut. You're not wearing thick trousers and heavy shoes in this hot weather. Sandals and shorts will be fine. Any stones on the lawn? Don't worry: this mower takes care of anything.

Now the damn thing's stalled. Often happens in heavy grass, even with rotaries. Soon clear it: just tilt the canopy and feel about underneath.

Having trouble with the electric mower? Probably the wet grass. Soon get those blades cleared. And don't waste time walking all the way back to the house to unplug the damn thing. Never get a pint at this rate.

Now, let's get weaving on this car. Perfectly safe: it's propped up on four 12-inch plant pots. Plenty of room to get underneath.

Cold in this garage. Shut those doors and put the heater on until the paint spraying's done. And then we can run the engine for a bit to see how she's performing. Oh, and check that battery. No need to disconnect the damn thing – just get on with it.

While we're here, let's siphon out some petrol for the lawn-mower. Anyone got a fag?

Burning the rubbish? Site the fire close to the house or the shed. Saves all that walking and doesn't make a mess of the lawn. Or if the wife's not keen on the smoke, stick it at the end of the garden: under the trees or by the hedge is just fine.

No need to fiddle about getting it started. Sling some petrol or paraffin on it. Leave the can near the fire in case it needs some more. And get rid of those empty aerosols while you're at it. Just sling 'em on. Adds to the fun.

Don't stand about feeding the fire: you've got more important things to do. Just chuck everything on at once – it'll soon burn down.

When darkness falls, don't bother raking out the fire and throwing water on the embers. It'll go out in its own good time. Looks like rain, anyway, what with the wind getting up like that.

The foregoing list is by no means exhaustive, and inventive do-it-yourselfers will have no trouble in finding a thousand other ways of speeding up the job. It's all good for trade, anyway. Ask any mortician.

CHAPTER SEVEN

A Halping Hand

A home handyman whose addiction to DIY is wrecking his marriage, ruining his career, or causing friends and neighbours to cut him dead in the street, need no longer despair.

All he has to do is contact the Handymen's Aids to Loafing Project, or HALP, whose skilled counsellors and special clinics are at his disposal to help overcome his craving. Today there is little stigma attached to the condition, nor need the patient worry about anyone finding out: treatment is all in the strictest confidence.

A patient at a typical HALP clinic is welcomed at the doorway (the door is leaning against the wall), and led upstairs (not relying too heavily on the banisters) into the Therapy Room. The first thing he realises, standing shoulder to shoulder with other sufferers, is that he is not alone. The incidence of addiction to DIY is increasing week by week, and his is far from a solitary vice.

There is no hanging about, no lengthy registration process. Treatment starts immediately with sedation by several large scotches, and the patient is encouraged to talk about the reasons for his problem.

Once he's got those off his chest – creative urges, need to save, artistic temperament, want to show that clever devil next door, nothing on the telly these days, at his age what else is there? – he already feels much better.

The next stage is to put the problem into its wider context, starting with a talk, illustrated with filmed interviews, on the anti-social effects of DIY. The patient sees long lines of honest and professional tradesmen put out of work and condemned to a life on the dole by his obsession. He sees the suffering endured by their wives, driven to distraction by having them under their feet all day. The poor ex-professionals do not even have DIY to help them pass the time, because they did it all years ago.

He sees the strain that compulsive do-it-yourselfers place on the social services by causing unnecessary work for already over-burdened medical staff. While the DIY men are in casualty being treated for nailing feet to the floor or sticking chisels through femoral arteries, some poor little mite has to wait outside for hours with his head stuck in a bucket or a set of metal railings clamped around his ears.

This is followed by real-life case histories of home handymen's wives. They tell their tragic stories of how they pleaded with their fanatical husbands to take up boozing, gambling, womanising – anything except DIY.

Perhaps the most harrowing scenes of all are those of innocent children being repressed and inhibited during their formative years. The most common word they hear is 'No', and they associate it thereafter with their father's activities. Listen to their plaintive wails as they are told, week after week:

'No! You can't go into the playroom. Daddy's making another recreational area.'

'No! You can't go into the living room. It's not fit to live in.'

'No! You can't go into the dining room while Daddy's wall-papering.'

'No! Your tea's not ready. Daddy's tiling the kitchen. Sit on the stairs quietly, or you'll go to bed without any junk food.'

'No! You can't go to bed early. Daddy's fixing some nice built-in wardrobes.'

'No! You can't watch television while Daddy's painting the ceiling.'

'No! You can't go out in the garden. Daddy's busy cementing. And *do* put that hammer drill down, darling. That's the third cat we've lost this month . . .'

After this, the patient is ready for group therapy. Former chronic do-it-yourselfers stand up one by one and tell the stories of their addiction and its sad consequences:

'I was in line for promotion until my DIY mania took its toll. Absenteeism, sickness, constantly falling asleep on the job; my hands stiff, cracked and raw, heavily bandaged, and now and again with another finger missing.

'One day my superior took me on one side. He said he was sorry to have to quibble, but inattention to detail and missing digits did constitute obstacles to the high standard of manual dexterity required in my line of work.

'It meant only one thing: demotion. I was taken off brain surgery straightaway and ever since have been fourth assistant swabber in the piles unit.'

. . . As the weeping former brain surgeon is led away, another man takes his place:

'I spent all my spare time at home making reproduction 18th-century inlaid escritoires. Work of the most delicate nature, it was, handling the most fragile of veneers. Though I say it myself, I turned out some of the most exquisite work, so faithful to detail that even Sotheby's accepted my work as genuine antiques.

'Of course, my professional life suffered. I was called into the office one day and the supervisor gave me my cards. Said my exhausted state had made me too clumsy to work on the dustbin round any more.'

. . . After him comes somebody looking even sadder. After a few desultory sniffs, he starts his story:

'I came into some money and bought myself a huge house. It was fine as it stood, really, but I couldn't leave well alone. I took out inside walls to enlarge the rooms, removed the old mullioned windows and replaced them with modern picture windows, and installed several dormer rooms in the lofts.

'There was plenty of room in the old place, but I would insist on adding extensions. I built new wash houses, outhouses, utility rooms, garages, mad-sister annexe, all that kind of stuff.

'Then one day the inevitable happened. The inside walls I'd taken out were load bearing, the larger windows I'd put in had weakened the outer structure, and the dormer rooms had weakened the lofts. The house caved in and caught fire. The fire brigade was not able to deal with the blaze properly because of the sprawl of outbuildings, and the whole place burned to the ground.

'I am now homeless and penniless, so if any of you would care to buy me a drink later, I wouldn't say no. The name's Usher, by the way: Roderick Usher . . .'

The next stage is aversion therapy. This intensifies genuine DIY sensations to the point where mind and body are revolted by the thought of lifting so much as a screwdriver.

The patient is taken into a large, bare-walled room, filled with a DIY version of white noise: the simultaneous sounds of hammer drills, sanders, polishers, planing machines, power saws and cement mixers. This noise is overlaid by loud exhortations in strident

Thatcherspeak to finish the job quickly, do it properly, and not leave any mess on the floor.

At regular intervals the patient is subjected to concentrated experiences of DIY sensations. His left thumb is placed against the wall and bashed rhythmically with a two-pound hammer. Bricks are dropped on his feet. Sensitive parts of his sensitive parts are jabbed with an assortment of sharp-pointed tools. Paint and hot roofing tar are poured down his neck.

After a five-minute break for therapeutic screaming, he is doubled up and forced into tiny enclosed spaces filled with waste traps, S-bends, U-bends, stopcocks, spiders, beetles and mice, while ice-cold water is dripped steadily onto his head and a choking dust pumped up his nose. On his release from this cramped and claustrophobic position, he is frogmarched over to a low beam, against which his head is banged (in three-four time) for several minutes.

He is then allowed a 10-minute rest period standing in a draught, and given a cup of cold tea, liberally laced with sawdust, plaster dust, cobwebs and dead flies. This is followed by a free-activity

period: he is taken to a bench on which lies an assortment of tools, and invited to pick up any tool to indulge in his favourite project. Each tool holds a little surprise: some carry an electric charge, some explode. The heavier ones come to pieces in his hands and drop on what's left of his feet. After several minutes he is disinclined to start any project, however much it used to take his fancy.

Comes the time for some real activity: painting the room. After what the patient has been through, the prospect comes as an immense relief. Until he is told that the room, which is 90 feet long, 50 feet wide and 14 feet high, has to be painted in one go, ceiling and all. With an undercoat and two topcoats. Oh, and to be cleaned down properly first.

To make sure he keeps at it, he is accompanied by one of HALP's more forceful rehabilitation agents, thrown out of the Mafia for brutality, who hits him with a sockful of pea shingle as soon as he starts to flag.

By the time he has finished the room – undercoat and two top coats, ceiling and all – he never wants to hear about another household job as long as he lives. All he wants to do is to get through that door into the outside world of sane and healthy pursuits (boozing, gambling, womanising, etc.) and leave his sordid DIY past behind.

He is almost there – just about to step across the threshold to freedom – when he is stopped by the rehabilitation agent, who has swapped his sockful of pea shingle for a pick handle with a spike through it.

'Just a minute,' says the agent. 'I don't like that colour. Do it again . . .'

HALP's activities are not confined to helping the compulsive do-it-yourselfer: it also looks after the dragooned DIY man, the one who hates every minute of it but who has been talked into it, nagged into it or physically forced into it by his wife.

Dragooning is very common, indeed accepted, in the early days of marriage, but over the years most husbands manage to find a way out. The weaker or more compliant ones, however, find themselves stuck with it. It seems as if there is no hope of reprieve: they have passed the point of no return. But have they?

HALP says no. There is still hope, however long any husband has knuckled under. All it needs is motivation – the will to break free – and some organisation.

The first step is to stiffen the will. Groups of the unfortunates –

Benching, Extending, Rendering and Kerfing Sufferers or BERKS for short – are gathered together for an initial morale-raising session under a cheer leader. The cheer leader chants questions and the BERKS shout back the answers, thus:

'Are you a mouse?'

'No!'

'Are you a toad?'

'No!'

'Are you a creep?'

'No!'

'Are you a man?'

'YES!'

With some sort of identity established, even if most of the BERKS still have their doubts, the cheer leader continues:

'Under her thumb?'

'No!'

'Tied to her apron?'

'No!'

'Frightened to death?'

'No!'

'Are you a man?'

'YES!'

By now the BERKS are starting to believe it, and it's time for the crunchers:

'What do we want?'

'More booze!'

'What do we get?'

'Do-it-yourself!'

'What do we want?'

'More telly!'

'What do we get?'

'Do-it-yourself!'

'What do we want?'

'Afternoon kip!'

'What do we get?'

'Do-it-yourself!'

'What of your wife?'

'To hell with the wife!'

'What of her mother?'

'To hell with her mother!'

'Are you a man?'

'Yes!'

'So what do we do?'

'DOWN TOOLS!'

The BERKS are now worked up to a white heat of courage and determination. Pausing only to don industrial masks and balaclava helmets to avoid identification, the stalwart lads march in protest through the town and picket the DIY shops. After which they make their way to the nearest pub to reinforce their resolve.

Results from this initial display of solidarity are not always lasting. By the time some of the BERKS get home, the booze has worn off and so has most of the courage. With others, although the courage remains, it does not stand up for long under the onslaught of tongue, rolling pin, coal shovel or flat iron.

But even those who knuckle under and meekly resume their paperhanging, are not yet lost. They are encouraged to report again for the more subtle DIY evasion courses: the Anti-Nagging Course, the Self-Defence Course, the Cock-It-Up Course, the Instant Disabilities Course and the Seen-To-Be-Done Course.

The Anti-Nagging Course is similar to the armed forces training to accustom recruits to the sound of gunfire. Getting used to it is all it boils down to. Take no notice, that's the secret.

The naggee reclines on a settee in front of the television, ashtray by his side, glass of beer in hand, and is subjected to verbal abuse from highly skilled professional naggers: large ladies chosen for their fearsome physique, power of lung and musculature of tongue.

With training, the naggee can sit motionless through the heaviest verbal barrage, responding only after half an hour or so to say: 'I'm sorry, my love. Did you speak?'

He allows the lady to let rip for another half hour, and then replies: 'Yerss . . . Quite a good match this afternoon, apart from that penalty. Would you mind saying that again, my dear? Going home to mother, you said? Give her my love, won't you . . .'

For the first couple of sessions at home, the naggee is advised to wear ear plugs and a hard hat. With practice, both can be discarded, but the hard hat only after he has become proficient in the techniques of self defence.

The Self-Defence Course starts by polishing up the patient's elementary survival techniques: diving behind the settee, locking himself in the broom cupboard or fleeing to the boozer. But thereafter it moves on to the skills of judo, karate, kung fu, and such western martial arts as kitchen-stool fighting, cat throwing and breadknife dodging.

The Cock-It-Up Course is more subtle, sophisticated and, until the wife learns to leave well alone and Get a Man In, incredibly expensive. But it works.

The patient agrees with every DIY project his Ever-Loving comes up with. Not only agrees with it, but launches into it with the greatest enthusiasm and even suggests additional things to tackle while he's got the doors off/floors up/roof off/wall down.

He invests in half a dozen expensive and specialist DIY tomes to ensure that he's working from the soundest and most up-to-date advice available, and refuses to buy anything but the best quality tools and material.

Then he begins, methodically and remorselessly, to cock things up.

The beginner can ease into it by practising a few basic cock-ups: punching a neat row of nail holes along the length of a concealed water pipe, or sawing through it along with the floorboards he's taking up; taking the washer out of a tap and then looking vainly for the stopcock (both operations much more effective when carried

out upstairs); dropping a large can of high-gloss white from a ladder onto the top of the stairs, on which he has recently laid a luxury Wilton and over which he has forgotten to lay any dust sheets.

He can discover for himself how easily shatterproof plate glass shatters when dropped from a height onto a concrete surface; how the same applies to roof- and wall-tiles.

Then he can attempt some more ambitious cock-ups.

It's surprising how difficult it is to unblock drains which have filled overnight with a creeping concrete mix; how far sloppy concrete will spread on a sloping site if the bottom boards of the formwork fail to stay in place; how easy it is to underestimate such materials as carpet tiles and discover that those stuck firmly to three-quarters of the floor were a discontinued line.

In time, assuming the cocker-up's Ever-Loving still trusts him to lift a hammer, he will have gained the experience and skill necessary for a super cock-up – which will bring down anything from a wall or ceiling to the whole house. Bringing down the whole house is a bit extreme and may be resented by his Ever-Loving, especially if she's inside it at the time. But it does ensure, one way or the other, that she never asks him to do a job again.

The Instant Disabilities Course gives instructions on faking symptoms of common or hitherto unheard-of afflictions which are severe enough to preclude the physical exertion or mental stress of DIY. Many of these afflictions are covered in the chapters 'Honestly Doctor: All I Did Was – Aaargh!' and 'All in the Mind', but they by no means constitute an exhaustive list.

A good medical dictionary will provide more afflictions than you could ever use, but make sure first that the cures do not involve anything drastic, such as giving up booze for life or having your leg off.

Common conditions popular among reluctant do-it-yourselfers include:

Bad back
Bad front
Flat feet
Rising arches
Falling arches
Short sight
Long sight
Tunnel vision
Double vision
High blood pressure
Low blood pressure
No blood pressure

Remember that halitosis, acne and sweaty feet do not rate high on the list of physical disabilities, and that dandruff is seldom terminal.

Sinus trouble or delicate lungs mean that you can't work in all that dust. And it's no use spraying water to lay the dust because you can't work in all that damp, either.

A bad hand is a good old standby, but (a) unless you're left-handed, make sure it's the right one, and (b) remember which one it's supposed to be. Beware of unwittingly revealing to your beloved that you can carry four pints of bitter from the bar in the allegedly afflicted mitt.

A good all-purpose exemption is the phrase, 'But the doctor told me . . .' Be prepared to counter the obvious objection with the reply, 'No, not *that* doctor – the sober one . . .'

If all else fails, break into an uncontrollable coughing fit and attempt to turn purple.

The Seen-To-Be-Done technique is quite painless for both parties and, indeed, keeps everybody happy. A wife is often content just to be aware of her husband busying himself around the house, and isn't always interested in inspecting the finished results.

The husband writes off for all the DIY catalogues and subscribes to a couple of home-improvement magazines, the covers of which he detaches and wraps around the latest *Playboy*.

He buys in a set of basic tools, a few bricks, a small bag of cement and a couple of buckets of sand. These are for leaving about where the wife will see them as evidence of work in progress. Better still, she will fall over them, and demand that he clear them away. Later, at the launderette, she can tell her friends proudly: 'My Sidney. I don't know, he's always under my feet with his do-it-yourself jobs around the house. I suppose I shouldn't complain, really . . .'

Sidney will further reinforce the image with evidence of what looks like work finished: a scattering here and there of sawdust, brick dust, plaster dust, mortar dust or just dust dust. The odd off-cut can be left around to show he's been sawing wood, then carefully collected and stored away for use again.

Outside confirmation of his efforts is provided by phone calls from his mates, enquiring after the progress of the latest job. When

speaking to the lady of the house, they do not specify which bit of the house the husband is supposed to be working on, but ask solicitously after his progress in coping with the problem of the rebate on the double-flanged inflow-pipe junction.

At this stage of the Seen-To-Be-Done operation, the husband may have to be fetched from his shed to answer the call. Though not strictly essential, a shed or garage is a handy base for non-operations. There, under cover of the noise of a bench saw, the husband may booze happily away while giving the occasional bash on a biscuit tin as a sign of more varied activity.

After the phone call, the husband can sigh about the difficulties involved in anything to do with double-flanged inflow-pipe junctions, and bemoan the fact that after all the blood, sweat, toil and tears, there's never a lot to show for it.

From the call, he now knows that his mates are down at the pub. It's time for the Leave-Me-To-It-I'm-A-Martyr-To-Home-Improvement routine. Diving into the cupboard under the stairs, he bangs about a bit, then chucks a few off-cuts, old screws and bits of plaster onto the hall carpet.

'Likely to be a bit messy, this, my love,' he says. 'Tell you what, why don't you go off and enjoy yourself down at the shops while I finish this off?'

As soon as she's gone, hubby chucks more mess about the hall – just in case she gets back before he does – then dives off to meet his mates in the boozer.

The Seen-To-Be-Done method has been described by objective observers as unethical, dishonest, underhanded, sly and a betrayal of marital trust.

It certainly has a lot going for it.

CHAPTER EIGHT

Honestly, Doctor: All I did was — Aaargh!

Do-it-yourself, although placing a great strain on hospital and casualty services, is constantly adding to the sum total of medical knowledge. Few other activities produce accidents and injuries in such profusion, variety and pottiness.

So it behoves casualty ward staff and newly-fledged GPs to be aware of some of the commoner manifestations of DIY injuries – compared to which, those sustained by high-wire clog dancers, hiccuping fire-eaters, one-armed dynamite jugglers and barefoot piranha trainers appear positively boring.

Though there is a steady stream of DIY casualties throughout the week, usually of the keener types who will never let well alone, Monday mornings see the biggest rush from those whose skills, co-ordination or brain-cell count were not up to the job in hand.

After the initial patching-up and sticking-back-on, medical staff need have no hesitation in giving the victims sick notes for time off work. Nobody who has been doing the things they have been doing, using the tools they have been using, standing on the things they were standing on, and knowing as little about the job as they did, should be allowed to associate with normal, sane people in any sort of work environment.

There is the danger that the sickee will use the spare time to take up the DIY operation where he left off and land himself back in casualty the following day. In which case the doctor is best advised to prescribe one of those unisex, unisize, back-to-front canvas jackets and stick him in a padded room under heavy sedation until he promises never to do it again.

Of course he will do it again: recidivism is one of the most marked traits of the compulsive do-it-yourselfer. And he'll keep turning up, though each time there'll be less and less of him, until something serious brings home the folly of his ways. For the real addict it has to be something extremely serious, such as death. But he can't say nobody warned him.

Shakin' All Over

Anybody brought in vibrating like Shakin' Stevens or the early Elvis has probably been working too long with a powered hedge trimmer, hammer drill or pneumatic drill. Don't expect to get much sense out of him unless you're an expert at morse code: all that emerges from between his chattering teeth is a sound like, 'Dah-dit-dah-dit . . .'

There's not a lot you can do for him until the vibrating has stopped naturally. Meanwhile you could put him to work sieving soil or shaking cocktails. Should the shaking persist, you could stick a couple of maracas in his hands and hire him out to the local Latin American combo.

What's This Ear?

One missing ear, known as the Van Gogh Syndrome, indicates that the patient was using a lightweight cordless jigsaw and stuck it behind his ear without turning it off. It is usually the left ear which is affected: his pencil is kept behind the right one.

Another common cause of ear loss is bending down over a bench

saw in an attempt to locate an irritating squeak. The loss of both ears – the Two Goghs Syndrome – can be caused by the patient's remembering that he was deaf in the first ear anyway, and bending down for another go.

You can try asking the patient whether he had the presence of mind to rescue one or both ears, but often the only answer you get is, 'Pardon?'.

Heads You Lose

Check before you attempt to treat anyone brought in with his head facing the wrong way. He may merely have put his jacket on back-to-front to protect his shirt from paint splashes.

Bear this in mind, too, when paint-splashed patients are brought in looking perfectly normal apart from being stone dead. Question the friend or neighbour who found him lying winded by the side of the tea chest or bucket on which he had been standing.

The answer may well be: 'I can't understand it, Doctor. He was perfectly all right until I turned his head the right way round.'

There is not a lot you can do for the victim, but the well-meaning first aider should be sent to have *his* head examined.

Down in the Mouth

A patient brought in with a three-inch paintbrush protruding bristles-first from the mouth has usually been painting a door. He had put the brush handle between his teeth to use both hands for something – and his wife walked in.

He may be accompanied by the dear lady who, depending on his reaction, could be suffering from severe cranial indentations consistent with being struck by a two-litre can of high gloss, or who could have a three-quarter-inch brush stuck up her left nostril.

Getting it Taped

A woman patient whose mouth is covered in masking tape has usually been offering advice or criticism at an inopportune moment, generally at the end of the day when the do-it-yourselfer has had enough of do-it-yourselfing.

The relationship of the tapee to the taper can often be determined by the width of the tape. For the average wife, 2-inch-wide tape is usually enough. A 3-inch width is the minimum for mothers-in-law.

Sometimes the tapee is a man. In which case it is a safe bet that his last recorded words were: 'I could be watching "World of Sport" now, instead of painting this – mmmpph . . .'

Stretching It a Bit

It is not uncommon for a DIY enthusiast to find himself with one

arm shorter than the other. If the shorter arm is digitally intact, however, it may be that he has one arm *longer* than the other.

A common cause is nailing the left sleeve accidentally to the eaves, and then kicking the ladder away in the struggle to get free. Should the arm not return to its normal length in the fullness of time, there's not a lot that can be done without major surgery. You could offer to put the other arm in traction until it's reached the same length, pointing out the DIY advantages of the longer reach.

After traction, the patient will need some rehabilitation therapy to accustom himself to the longer arms. He must overcome any inclination to chest beating, over-indulgence in bananas and impure thoughts about Fay Wray. He will also have to relearn his spatial co-ordination if he is not to keep painting the semi next door or picking the nose of the man next to him.

Thinking Small

The patient arrives with eyes bleary, watering and blinking. His hands are trembling violently and making vague wandering movements, as if he's trying to find the right keys on a piano.

He may be muttering, 'Blues . . . Where did I put the blues? Can't finish the sea without the blues . . . And where are those gold bits? There's a hole in my Mediterranean sunrise . . .'

He's almost certainly an over-ambitious mosaic enthusiast, daft enough to try an intricate pattern with individual stones, instead of buying the stuff in sheets and just slapping it down.

Confirm diagnosis by producing a few colour-blindness charts and asking him to pick out the numbers among the differently coloured dots. Ignore the screams.

Hairy Scary

The patient is brought in wild-eyed, twitching and gibbering, and you discover that his snow-white hair turned like that overnight. This is the man who built an extension on his garage and discovered too late that he'd bricked himself in. Not a lot you can do for him, except prescribe a sedative and a course of Grecian 2000.

The same traumatic effects can be brought about by working in a cellar, especially the cellar of a very old house. Either he was locked in overnight, or he discovered something strange under the pile of rubble in the corner.

Should he be carried in by a large gentleman in stack boots, ill-fitting clothes, with a stiff-legged gait and green complexion, do not be alarmed: that was probably what he found under the rubble.

The large gentleman himself may need some attention: 'It's these bolts in my neck, Doctor. They're rusting something chronic.'

If you haven't any easing oil in the surgery, direct him to the nearest ironmonger. Should the nearest ironmonger be brought in, wild-eyed, twitching and gibbering, perhaps you should have phoned first.

King Pong

He is covered in an evil-smelling brown sludge and was deposited outside the surgery by firemen who knocked on the door and ran away. He is the do-it-yourselfer who decided to clean out the cesspit – and fell in. The family was probably not at home. When cesspits are being cleaned, few families are.

Initial treatment is simple: leave him outside and hose him down through the letter-box.

His treatment thereafter will be mainly psychological to rid him of the effects of total social deprivation. For several days after the event, no matter how thoroughly he has been hosed, he will be thrown off buses, ejected from pubs and ostracised by his family, assuming they've dared to come back. Even his best friends won't tell him.

If you are treating him as a private patient, make sure you get your money first. Anybody who cleans out his own cesspit is either as tight as a duck's wotsit or broke to the wide.

High-de-High

The patient is in a state verging on the ecstatic: giggling, laughing, perhaps singing or dancing, and attempting to make passionate love to your receptionist whether she's 20, trim and tasty, or 50, fat and frosty.

He has left behind him a half-finished job about which his wife is complaining bitterly. Psychedelic sunbursts painted all over the living room ceiling are something she could live without.

Check his utterances. If he is mumbling such phrases as, 'Too much . . . Way out . . . Laid back, man . . .' he has been working with thinners, glues or solvents in a confined space and is, in medical terminology, bombed out of his brains.

Stand him in a draught, give him a few deep breathing exercises, and tell him not to do it again. He'll be in enough trouble as it is when his wife collects him. She will definitely not approve of that spiky green Mohican haircut and the bondage chains around his knees.

Perhaps his appearance is normal and it's just his behaviour that is erratic: stumbling gait, slurring of words and a tendency to burst into song. Should the songs be such closing-time favourites as *Delilah, Nellie Dean* and *We'll Meet Again*, suspect the Demon Drink.

A check with his wife will probably reveal that he's been nowhere near a pub. Never touches a drop. He's been locked away in his shed all morning, working hard on his latest project.

A further check will probably reveal that his wife decided to help the project along by re-filling some near-empty bottles she discovered in the shed: bottles marked Methylated Spirits, Surgical Spirits and Industrial Alcohol. Which she filled with methylated spirits, surgical spirits and industrial alcohol. Not realising that the labels were code for whisky, gin and white rum, a favourite ruse of shed-haunting husbands who Never Touch a Drop.

After a few swigs at each bottle, puzzling over the flavour and the fact that there seemed to be more in the bottles than he remembered, the husband would have been well past caring and supped the lot.

Do not give the game away to his wife. She wouldn't thank you for it. Neither would he, by the time she'd finished with him. Put his condition down to a build-up of fumes. And tell him in future to keep the genuine booze at the bottom of his tool chest. At least in future you'll know where to call for a stiff one when the pubs are shut.

Concrete Proposals

Concrete is a regular feature of DIY accidents, and a brief

observation of the patient will tell you how he came to have what he's got and why it's where he's got it.

A person totally coated in concrete and spinning like a top is someone who had the bright idea of standing on a bench to fill the mixer from above, and who failed to ensure that the bench top was non-slip. Try to stop him spinning before he screws himself into the ground.

You can confirm your initial diagnosis by ascertaining if he is suffering from dizziness and nausea, symptoms of spending even the briefest time in a revolving mixer. Make absolutely sure, though, that he understands the question. If you ask simply, 'Have you vertigo?', he is likely to reply, 'No. I only live round the corner.'

A person set solid in a large block of cement is the do-it-yourselfer who rushed out to redirect the dumping of a load of ready-mixed. The driver failed to notice him as he stood behind the mixer yelling, 'Left hand down a bit!'

Someone brought in soaking wet, covered in duckweed, perhaps with the odd frog in his pocket and with both feet set firmly in a tub of cement, has been recovered from the local canal. This man is likely to be a fanatical, seven-day-a-week do-it-yourselfer. Both the tub of cement and the trip to the canal were by courtesy of his nextdoor neighbour, who had finally snapped under the non-stop drilling, hammering and banging.

If the canal were deep enough and he had been in there long enough, the patient could be in a really serious condition, i.e. dead. In which case it is hardly worth chipping him free. Other patients in the waiting room can pass the time happily by pushing him over and watching him bob up again.

Creature Discomforts

DIY is no occupation for anyone not fond of animals, especially little ones. Work on lofts, roofs, cellars and in the garden disturbs the poor things and deprives them of food and shelter. They've got to go somewhere, and they've got to eat. Often they take shelter on the body of the do-it-yourselfer. And often they take the odd piece out of him.

In the case of a severe phobia, the creatures need not even exist except in the mind of the sufferer. So if you get a distraught loft-converter leaping into the surgery shouting, 'Doctor! Doctor! I'm covered in hairy green things with twelve legs, three heads and poison fangs!' your first duty is to calm him down and assure him that the creatures are purely figments of his imagination. Meanwhile, tell him not to brush the bloody things off all over you.

Imaginary creatures, however, are more the province of

psychiatry than medicine (see the chapter 'All in the Mind'). Your main concern is with real creatures which take refuge on the do-it-yourselfer.

The smaller creatures will take refuge anywhere: in hair, in ears, up sleeves and nostrils and down shirts. The danger is greatest, though, and the effect on the host most traumatic when the animal is a little larger and the refuge is sought up a trouser leg. Health services would be saved an enormous amount of money every year if only more home handymen would wear bicycle clips.

Mice are not too much trouble, providing they have not been in the trousers long enough to start breeding. They can be dealt with by:

(a) Lowering a baited trap on a piece of string down inside the waistband;

(b) Inserting a small-to-medium-sized cat;

(c) Having the do-it-yourselfer remove his socks in the hope that the smell of simulated gorgonzola will tempt the mice out of hiding.

Most hosts prefer the sock-removal method. Baited traps can be sprung by the slightest contact, and not all cats can see too well in the dark.

Dormice can be dangerous in autumn. After a few minutes up the trouser leg, they are likely to hibernate in the host's Y-fronts.

Extreme care must be taken in removing them: should they be woken up suddenly they are likely to take a bite out of the nearest object.

Rats, of course, are the worst threat to the handyman's body and peace of mind, and for these the only answer is a ferret. Put the ferret up one trouser leg and make sure that the end of the other trouser leg is propped wide open. A cornered rat will fight to the death, and in the restricted space there could be a great deal of incidental damage. But providing it can see light at the end of the tunnel, it should leave quickly if not quietly.

It is best to tie a piece of string to the ferret's hind leg: it might take a liking to the place once the rat's gone, and there's nothing you can send up to chase out a ferret.

The most painful invasion of all is by a hedgehog. Its spines point in all directions, so whichever way it moves it makes its presence felt. The only safe way of removal is to cut a large piece out of the front of the trousers, lift out the hedgehog bodily, and hope the patient doesn't meet anybody on the way home. Porcupines would be much less painful to remove because their spines all point one way, but porcupines are too big to get up trouser legs. Silly to mention them really.

There has been no record so far, at least in temperate climes, of a boa constrictor finding its way up a home handyman's trouser leg, but there soon may be. A friend of the author lost the constrictor he was looking after for a neighbour. In Hemel Hempstead, Hertfordshire, it was.

The likelihood was that it finished up seeking warmth from somebody's central heating system. So if anyone in Hemel Hempstead is doing things to the pipes and feels something cold and scaly sliding up his trouser leg . . .

Seriously, he needn't worry too much. Boa constrictors are not poisonous. All they can do is crush you to death.

Game, Set and Scratch

This man has the lot: the classic DIY multi-purpose injury. It has happened before and it will happen again, though nobody ever believes it when it does.

The victim:

Has severe lacerations to the chest and knees, all three of which are impregnated with brick dust, tile dust or slate flakes, gravel and bits of tarmacadam;

Often clutches a paint brush in his right hand and a broken piece of guttering in his left;

Has bits of herbaceous or shrubbery plants in his hair, along with a bird's nest or two;

Has a nose which is either severely flattened or swollen to prizewinning tomato size;

Has a frayed piece of rope tied around his waist.

What happened was that he felt unsafe at the top of the ladder as he was painting the guttering, and decided to secure himself by tying a rope round his waist. He could find nothing on which to knot the other end of the rope so he threw it over the roof and, on the other side, tied it to the nearest solid object: the rear bumper of the family car.

As he painted happily away, his wife got into the car and drove off, dragging him off the ladder, up the roof, down the other side, through the herbaceous borders, up the drive and out into the road.

This man is often very distraught on arrival. As is his wife, to whom he has addressed some very naughty words. Before treatment, therefore, it is essential to calm both parties down.

Assure the wife that these things happen in the best of families, and that a bent back bumper will cost very little to straighten out: in fact it could be done for nothing by her handyman husband, once he's out of intensive care.

Congratulate the husband on his choice of colour for the paint – ensuring first that you are not admiring the blood – and on the prettiness of the blooms in his hair: dahlias are never as easy to grow as most people think.

Treat the wife for shock and send her home. Treat the husband for lacerations, contusions and galloping stupidity, but not before you have called together any available consultants, housemen and students: it could be years before they saw another mess like this.

Swinging the Lead

It is inevitable that, among the genuine sufferers, there will be the occasional malingerer, whose symptoms are faked and whose only concern is to be graded officially unfit for DIY, preferably for life.

Such an attempt at malingering is a Cry for Help – the last resort of an exhausted mind and body – so it would be no betrayal of the Hippocratic Oath to grant the skiver the exemption he craves. But by the same Oath you are bound to see through the pretence and arrive at a correct diagnosis.

The most commonly faked symptoms are Bad Eyes, Bad Ears, Bad Legs and Bad Backs.

The Bad Eyes case walks in wearing dark glasses, tapping a white stick in front of him, and falls over the proferred chair.

'I'm going blind, Doctor,' he sobs, addressing the skeleton hanging in the corner. 'It could be snow blindness from all this white paint I'm using. Or myopia from trying to read the instructions on those self-assembly three-piece suites that any child can put together in half an hour. Or perhaps it's the fumes from the varnish I'm using on the stairs.

'It's not just the prospect of spending the rest of my life falling over things that worries me: it's affecting my work. Three times this week I've run down an inspector before I've even got the bus out of the depot.'

'There, there,' you say, reassuringly. 'I'm sure it's nothing serious. Just look at that chart over there.'

'What chart?'

'On the wall.'

'What wall?'

Here you have a really determined case. But proceed. Let him stand a couple of feet away from the chart and fail to make out even the huge letter H at the bottom. Then back him away to the far side of the room, still facing the chart, which you now flick over to reveal a *Playboy* centrefold.

A genuine case of failing sight continues to stare blankly. The malingerer cries. 'Phwarh! Just look at those! Pet of the Month for June, eh? And according to the caption she's only . . .'

Deafness, usually blamed on noise from power tools, is easier to simulate.

'Good morning,' you greet the patient.

'Pardon?'

'And what seems to be the trouble?'

'Yes. Shocking for this time of year.'

'I mean, what can I do for you?'

'Half past eleven.'

But it's even easier to spot the fake.

Walk to your bookshelf and study the titles with your back to the patient. Then whisper, 'Actually, I was just going to nip out to the pub. Fancy a pint?'

Replies such as, 'Ready when you are, Doc!', 'Now you're talking,' and 'Lead me to it!' indicate not even a modest degree of hearing impairment. And if he's at the door before you are, note that there's nothing wrong with his legs, either, just in case he's saving those for his second line of attack.

Similar techniques can be used on the Bad Leg and Bad Back cases. Listen sympathetically to Bad Leg, prescribe him something harmless, ask him to call back in a couple of days, and consult your watch.

'Pity I've got more patients to see,' you say, casually. 'I'll have missed it.'

'Missed what?'

'Happy Hour at the Red Lion down the road. Promotional stunt. They're giving away free beer, as much as you can drink. But the offer ends in 10 minutes.'

However slowly and painfully the patient leaves the surgery, observe him as he gets out into the road. If he jumps into the air, clicks his heels together and takes off like a rocket, his leg was possibly not giving him as much trouble as he indicated.

A Bad Back is the trickiest. It is difficult to prove by normal diagnostic methods the patient's degree of pain, if any. And a Bad Back is easier to fake than a Bad Leg, in that a malingerer does not have to remember on which side he's supposed to be limping.

In he shuffles, on two sticks, and lowers himself into the chair, bent almost double.

'It was that concreting that did it, Doctor,' he winces. 'I should never have –'

'Yes, yes. I understand. But you'll be glad to hear that I'm experimenting with a new treatment: 12-year-old Scotch. Half a bottle a day. It's not on prescription yet, but I'm giving away trial quantities. Now, if you'll just reach me that bottle on the top shelf behind you . . .'

Buddy, Can You Spare a Part?

The increase in DIY over recent years has led to great advances in spare-part surgery techniques. It has to be accepted, however, that because of the nature of some of the injuries, there are not always enought bits left to go round. Out of 10 severe cases it is often possible to cobble together no more than four or five handymen who are fully operational and have the requisite number of appendages.

This calls for some consultation about which wife gets what. Ten wives into five husbands won't go, even though between them the five husbands are sharing bits from the original 10.

The burden of choice is an awesome one to place on the surgeon. Whatever he decides, there are bound to be five disappointed women. And even those whose husbands are restored to them are likely to complain:

'Yes, I *know* he looks like my Sidney in parts. Same bandy legs. Same tattoo on his chest – *Sidney Loves Violet, True*, beneath a couple of hearts entwined – and the same mole on his little bottom, bless him. But my Sidney wasn't Chinese . . .'

There can be trouble, too, when one bereft spouse notices that some particularly striking piece of her husband's anatomy, perhaps the only bit left in working order, has been grafted onto the man handed over to another woman:

'She's not taking him away with *that* attached! Belonged to my Lurch, that did – I'd recognise it anywhere! His pride and joy, that was; the envy of every man in the DIY Discount Centre. So take it off at once! If nothing else I can have it varnished and keep it on the shelf he was putting up just before his accident.'

Reactions such as these have shown that even a sturdy right kneecap can have its sentimental value.

Perhaps a fairer way is to let the women choose among themselves: either fight for it, toss for it, or take it in turns on a rota system. Even on the rota system there will still be the occasional squabble. A reconstructed husband may be kept too long at one house to make the fullest use elsewhere of his newly-found paper-hanging skills. And when the next wife in line eventually gets him back, she may discover that the transplants have absolutely ruined him for his old speciality of bricklaying:

'You've only been working on that garden screen for three days and already the council have got an order for its demolition. You're not the man I married, Cyril Higginson . . .'

She could be nearer the truth than she realises. The man she married, or bits of him, could be busy painting the living room three doors down.

Another alternative is to let the men make the choice, but this has proved even less successful.

In some cases the do-it-yourselfers have refused to go back to

wives who by this time are only partly theirs anyway, or to household jobs which got them into this mess in the first place. Instead they have rushed straight to the pub to celebrate their new-found freedom.

In other cases in which there are nine matronly, respectable, houseproud wives and one blonde and beautiful nymphomaniac with no interest at all in DIY, the reconstructed men have all gone for the blonde and beautiful nymphomaniac. In the absence of any logical cause for such a response, investigating psychiatrists have put it down to post-operational trauma, pending results of in-depth interviews on emotional transference with the lady concerned. So far, none of the interviewing psychiatrists has reported back.

CHAPTER NINE

All In The Mind

There is nothing more satisfying, fulfilling, productive, creative and money-saving than the noble art of self-sufficiency. So why does the very thought of it bring you out in spots? The answer is probably a phobia.

A phobia, as doubtless you know, is a dislike, morbid fear, horror or unreasoning dread of something. It may be mice, spiders, crowds, tax forms – anything. There is no justification for it at all in logic; no basis for it at all in actuality. But that does not make its effects any less real: the very lack of reason makes it terrifying for the sufferer and very difficult to treat. Even the symptoms of it are apparent only when the afflicted one comes face-to-face with the object of dread. You could be riddled with phobias you don't even know you've got.

All of which makes phobias very handy things to have. You can have as many as you like: there's one for almost every job and to suit every pocket. They're easy to apply, undetectable when not in use, simple to maintain, and with proper care should last a lifetime.

The basic rules of phobia maintenance are (a) remember that you've got one and react accordingly at the appropriate times, and (b) don't choose one which might restrict other activities.

You could, for instance, have *nelophobia*, which is a morbid fear of glass and which is guaranteed to get you excused all glazing jobs. But it is hard to explain why glass in sheets gives you the screaming heebies when you can face a whole row of glasses in the pub without so much as a twitch.

Let's look, then, at some of the phobias which afflict do-it-yourselfers. (Keep these pages by you for easy reference. You never know when you might need them.)

Work outdoors can be affected by *agoraphobia* (fear of open spaces). Your Nearest and Dearest may attempt to cure this by putting you in blinkers or sticking a paper bag over your head. This might allay your fears about space a little, but it does leave you prone to falling off and bumping into things, and doesn't do your bricklaying a lot of good. Nor is it any defence against fears of the weather out in the open.

The slightest breeze could bring on your *ancraophobia* (fear of wind). Atmospheric wind, that is: nothing to do with the curry and mushy peas you ate last night.

A nip in the air could strike you down with *cheimatophobia* (fear of cold), complicated by *cryophobia* (fear of ice or frost). A darkening of the sky means that *nephophobia* (fear of clouds) is on its way, closely followed by *brontophobia* (fear of thunder), *antlophobia* (fear of floods), or *chionophobia* (fear of snow).

Foggy weather will have you shaking with *homichlophobia*, not to mention the *hygrophobia* brought on by the attendant dampness (do not confuse this with *hydrophobia*, which is dealt with later).

The sun's come out? That's no consolation. Not with your allergy to strong light, or *photophobia* as it's known in the trade. Nor is it any use trying to escape by working outdoors at night. Anywhere in the world you could be afflicted by *siderophobia* (fear of the stars). Not only that, but in extreme northern and southern latitudes, a severe dose of *aurorophobia* (fear of auroral lights) could make your eyes go funny.

It is possible to avoid the extreme effects of night and day by getting up at dawn. Or it would be if that didn't bring on galloping *eosophobia*. Even working at dusk isn't the answer, as the gathering dark is bound to bring out your *nyctophobia*. And if you believed in ghosts you could have a bad attack of *phasmophobia*.

Working above ground level is definitely out. Fear of heights, *altophobia*, could set in anywhere above the first rung of the ladder. The fear alone could make you overbalance and prove you weren't kidding about your fear of gravity, or *barophobia*.

Should you finish your fall below ground level, such as in the excavations for your new footings, you could expire from *bathophobia*, which sounds like an aversion to soap and water but is actually a fear of depths.

As for drains and gutterings – Eeuch! The feel, or the very sight, of slime lays you wide open to *blennophobia* and *myxophobia*. Two for the price of one is bad enough, but they are usually allied to *bacillophobia*, a fear of all those germs lurking there, and the consequent fear of disease, *pathophobia*. Should you want to make it five, you could throw in the other fear of disease, *nosophobia*.

What's the difference between *blennophobia* and *myxophobia*, and *pathophobia* and *nosophobia*? Don't ask. Just be glad you've got 'em.

'Forget the outside jobs, then,' says your Loved One. 'Just do this little job under the sink and then see to that lagging in the loft.'

No way. Is your Loved One not aware of your *claustrophobia*, the fear of enclosed spaces, and one of the commonest of phobic afflictions? Does she not realise also that the dust in either location could have you coughing yourself to death with *amathophobia*? And that certainly in the loft you may be frightened out of your wits by spiders (*arachnophobia*), non-specific insects (*entomophobia*), birds (*ornithophobia*) and mice (*musophobia*). It matters little that they may be dead: the effect could be even worse by bringing on your *necrophobia*. If there's anything you hate, it's corpses. Even bits of the deceased could cause *doraphobia* (fear of fur) or *pteronophobia* (fear of feathers). There's no phobia yet for bits of defunct spider, but just give it time.

That work under the sink could have you seizing up and possibly foaming at the mouth with *hydrophobia*, the dreaded fear of water. On second thoughts, it might be risky to claim you have hydrophobia. Should the doctor be busy and the vet called in instead, he could do no more than put you down. ('Kindest thing in the end. Save all that suffering. And he's had a good run . . .')

Some people like to be left alone when they're working, but as you are suffering from *eremitophobia*, the fear of being on your own, you've got another very good reason for not squeezing under the sink or into the loft. And that's quite apart from *anginophobia*, the fear of narrowness.

'Very well, then,' your Loved One replies. 'You can go down to the DIY shop and get the materials for the next job. You won't be on your own there.'

No, you certainly won't. The place is usually packed. And though you don't like being on your own, you also suffer from intermittent *demophobia*, which makes you go all to pieces in a crowd.

Perhaps you could just sit down quietly and read a DIY manual? You'd love to, except that your *bibliophobia* gives you a horror of books.

Just paint that wall, then. Eek! And come out in *chromophobia*, the morbid fear of colour? Apart from the paint fumes bringing on your *toxiphobia*, a fear of poison, which can be triggered off also by solvents, adhesives and paint strippers.

Something more basic? Knock in a nail? Screw in a screw? Not

when you're suffering from *aichurophobia* (bless you!) a dread of things pointed. The slightest mishap with either and your fear of pain – the dreaded *algophobia* (not to mention your fear of injury, *traumatophobia*) – would be totally justified. And should there be blood, you'd be reduced to a gibbering wreck with *haematophobia*.

Change a plug? How could you, with your *elektrophobia*? Apart from the fear of being fried, you are also terrified at the prospect of the mildest shock, a feeling which anyone suffering from *hormephobia* will fully understand.

Hang a mirror? Not with your *eisoptrophobia*, which is a variation on the fear of ordinary glass and shows that you're a true specialist.

Wherever you turn, there's bound to be some physical exertion involved. Whatever kind it is, it is bound to result in *kopophobia*, an aversion to fatigue.

Take some of the strain out of things, then, by using power tools.

Dear me, no. Not with your *mechanophobia* and *metallophobia*, fears of machinery and metals. And any kind of soldering, welding, or heat-based operation is ruled out by your *thermophobia*.

Your Nearest and Dearest may point out that two phobias you don't seem to have are *thaasophobia*, the dread of sitting idle, and *potophobia*, an aversion to drink. So how come you've got all the others? Including simple *kinetophobia*, a fear of getting into motion?

Explain that perhaps the responsibility of all these household jobs weighs too heavily on you, causing severe *hypegiaphobia*, a horror of carrying the can. That your *atelophobia* gives you a revulsion against anything short of perfection. That subconsciously you fear failure and ridicule, resulting in *kakorraphiaphobia* and *katagelophobia*. That you fear many things, causing severe *polyphobia*. And that you even fear being afraid, which brings on your *phobophobia*.

You are frightened of producing a pleasing result because the mildest praise would make you blush, a condition which your *erythrophobia* causes you to dread.

. . . The foregoing collection of phobias should convince even the most sceptical. Should it not, and should your most sceptical Nearest and Dearest accuse you of *ergophobia**, take no notice. Why, you've never heard of such a thing. Which is not surprising, as you are unlikely to take the trouble to look it up.

* A morbid fear of work, it is. Bloody cheek.

CHAPTER TEN

Next To Godliness

The bathroom is something you can be thinking about. Not *doing* anything about, just thinking about.

The bathroom is supposed to be the Room of the Eighties. By the time the designers have finished sorting it out, it might just be in time for its debut as the Room of the Nineties.

The bathroom, as we know it, is obsolete. Its current size and design in most houses evolved to cope with a few specific and limited private functions and is based on strict Victorian taboos. The result is that most bathrooms are too small, badly designed and almost totally inadequate for the demands of life a century later.

A team of Italian architects addressed themselves to the production of a bathroom for the year 2000. (See? Already you can forget the Eighties. And the Nineties.) They came up with fifty-seven associated activities which ought to be provided for.

They discovered, for instance, that taking medicines was linked to washing hands; vomiting was often followed by cleaning the teeth; getting dressed or undressed was linked with cutting toe nails, and exercise was followed by a relaxation session. The bathroom, they further concluded, was a much more logical place in which to wash, iron and store clothes, than the kitchen. And there were many other activities which people could share, all of which ought to take place in the bathroom.

The Italians are not alone in their thinking. Designers the world over have been looking at the bathroom, and adding to it such functions as laundry, library, conservatory, rest room and recreation centre. The place is on the verge of becoming as public as

Piccadilly Circus or Times Square, and for that it needs space and a complete rethinking of what used to be considered private functions.

Communal activities in bathrooms are not new. The Romans bathed together, as do the Japanese. The Romans did other things together, too, as can be deduced from the communal loo discovered at Pompeii. People just sat around, chatting and presumably borrowing each others' copies of the *Pompeii Thunderer* to catch up on the day's news. Toilet paper as we know it did not exist in Roman times, however – vellum and parchment being not only expensive, but a bit on the abrasive side – and a feature of the Pompeii loo was a sponge on a stick which was passed around as the need arose. It paid to go early.

In Britain, until Victorian times, people went to the loo publicly and in mixed sexes. There were communal family loos in Britain and America, with smaller holes in the bench seats for the kids. Then Thomas Crapper produced the one-at-a-time flush loo which was installed in a little brick shack outside, or a tiny room inside. The bath, too, when it replaced the portable zinc one which was used in front of the kitchen fire on Friday nights, was stationed in a little room with a lock on the door. Victorian prudery had set in.

This led to the whole syndrome of ablutions being shrouded in secrecy and carried out one at a time. It also fed the music hall joke industry with such gems as:

'We're all good singers in our family. We have to be – there's no lock on the bathroom door.'

And:

A teacher asked the class of six-year-olds if anybody knew where God lived.

'Please Miss,' said little Susie. 'He lives in our bathroom.'

'Whatever makes you think that?' asked the teacher.

'Well, Miss, every morning my daddy bangs on the bathroom door and says, "God! Are you going to be in there all day?"'

. . . Plumbing brought with it a whole new set of mysteries and complications which the amateur handyman has ever since found difficult to cope with. There was the handyman who installed an early bidet, the operation of which was at best erratic. His wife named it Old Faceful.

Then there was the man who was trying to clear a blocked drain with a set of rods. As there were several drains leading off the trap, he wasn't sure which one was at fault.

Anyhow, he persevered, and after pushing several yards of rodding into the third drain, he definitely felt some resistance. 'This is it,' he thought, and shoved away manfully.

After a couple of minutes he was tapped on the shoulder by his nextdoor neighbour.

'Would you mind trying another drain?' asked the neighbour. 'You've had my missis out of the bath twice.'

One allegedly true story was about the guest at a country house who went for a bath before dinner and forgot to lock the door.

The lady of the house, rounding up the guests and assuming it was her husband who was in the bath, walked in to find a naked male form, dimly discernible through the steam, bending over in the bath with its back to her.

She reached her hand through its legs, tugged at what approximated to a bell-pull, and cried: 'Ding ding! Dinner's ready!'

The form straightened up. 'Thank you, madam,' replied the guest. 'I'll be down directly.'

Generally speaking, royalty and the upper classes had fewer inhibitions about their toilet. Several European monarchs were in the habit of receiving their courtiers as they sat enthroned on the loo; the forerunner of the working breakfast, though on such an occasion breakfast was furthest from anybody's thoughts.

The French revolutionary leader Marat used to receive visitors as he sat in his bath, and this eventually brought him to an untimely end at the hands of Charlotte Corday, who was peeved about something or other. It must have come as quite a surprise to him: she seemed such a *nice* girl:

'Ah, bonjour Charlotte, ma cherie. Be with you in a minute. Put that knife down and pass me the rubber duck, there's a good – Aaargh!'

Anyway, get the picture? The bathroom of the future will no longer be a private place. Many of the activities, new and old, for which it is used, will take place in the presence of others: mainly members of the household, but also friends, tradesmen and perhaps the odd passing stranger. This will mean a big room, and, if all the proposed functions are to be exercised, possibly the whole top floor of the average house.

The only private function will be that of excretion, or Big Jobs as they say in design circles, and even then it will not be in conditions of complete privacy. The loo will be tucked into a cubicle in one corner, allowing the sittee to join in the social chit-chat going on in the rest of the place.

As an aid to thought on the subject, let's project a scenario of the likely activities in the Bathroom of the Future, and see how they could be combined on a typically busy morning:

The first job is to fight your way through the rampaging indoor plants, water the Fiddle-leaf Fig, wipe down the leaves of the

Umbrella Tree, genuflect to the Prayer Plant, slash back the weekend's growth of the Busy Lizzie, and make sure your dressing gown is adjusted before you approach the Venus Fly Trap.

The whirlpool bath is already in operation, with protruding snorkels and wave-tossed inflatable Snoopy dogs indicating that the kids are in there somewhere.

The door to the loo cubicle is locked. 'Good morning,' you shout.

'Morning,' replies the house guest from inside. 'Nice day. Hope you don't mind: I've borrowed *War and Peace* from the shelf. Nice library you've got here.'

Exercise first. Ten minutes' energetic sculling on the rowing machine, a short weight training session with the wall gym, then into the shower.

A bit crowded in the shower. 'Ours was packed with relatives,'

explains the girl from next door, soaping herself vigorously, 'so I just popped round. Didn't think you'd be up so early.

'Oh, this is Darren, my boyfriend – say hello, Darren. He was a bit shy of sharing our shower with Auntie Ellen, so I brought him with me. Anyway, do come in; there's plenty of room. Pass the loofah, Darren, there's a pet.'

Before stepping in, make sure that there are no pets, apart from Darren, sharing the shower. After avoiding the Venus Fly Trap, it would be a shame to be brought low by a shortsighted snapping turtle.

Finish ablutions, clean teeth and have a shave, jostling for position at sink with Darren and his beloved. Omit to vomit, as is provided for in the bathroom plans: don't want to upset the young people. Not that Darren seems to have any such inhibitions. Feeling better now, Darren?

What now? Cut toenails and relax in armchair for rest period, taking down from shelf a copy of *Hard Times*. Nothing like a spot of culture first thing in the – 'Ah, good morning, dear.'

Enter wife with laundry basket. She fills washing machine, whose noise thankfully drowns the rumblings and apologies from the loo. However, she has to turn up the record player very loud for the aerobics music to be heard abover the washer.

Aerobics over, wife jumps into whirlpool bath which the kids have now vacated in favour of disco roller skating to aerobics music.

Door opens and in walks the milkman.

'Good morning, missis,' he says to the wife. 'I've left the usual three pints, but we've got some spuds on special offer. And did you want any double cream?'

Order completed – one bag of spuds, two cartons double cream – milkman exits. Pausing only to compliment wife on recent weight loss – 'Must be that whirlpool bath' – and to give an appreciative 'Phwarh!' to the girl from next door who is currently vibrating in a slenderising machine.

Door opens again and in walks the vicar, smiling benignly, nodding to wife in whirlpool bath, to girl-next-door, and to Darren, who is flexing Neanderthal muscles in front of full-length mirror.

'Good morning, good morning, good morning,' beams the vicar, his glasses misting up in the steam.

'Good morning, vicar,' choruses everybody, except the kids who crash into him on their roller skates, and the house guest who can't hear a thing over the aerobics music and who is still immersed in *War and Peace*.

The vicar picks himself up and crosses the room, picking himself up again after falling over the ironing board.

'Good morning again, dear lady,' he says, wiping the mist from his specs and addressing the whirlpool bath with intense pastoral interest. 'I wondered if I might take you up on your offer of facilities for our Boys' Brigade. You remember how concerned I was about the lack of space in our church hall and you said – Ah, thank you, dear lady.'

'Right, boys! By the front, qui-ick MARCH!'

In marches the Boys' Brigade drill squad, preceded by the band, executing some very smart parade ground manoeuvres, marred only by the occasional crash into the washing machine, ironing board, vibrating girl-next-door and your own dear self. Plus the splash from the drum major who, in trying to follow the flight of his mace, lands in the whirlpool bath with the wife.

'Always been a tricky movement, that,' he says.

By this time you've had enough. *Hard Times* is right. Forgetting the rules of Bathroom 2000 hospitality, you leap from the armchair and eject vicar, Boys' Brigade, drum major, kids and young lovers, and pound on the door of the loo.

'You've been in there an hour!' you bellow to the house guest. 'Haven't you finished yet?'

'Fraid not, old chap,' comes the reply. 'Some book, this, I'm only up to Chapter Three . . .'

You can see, then, the problems involved in planning the Bathroom of the Future. Which is why, until the designers have ironed out a few of the snags, you are best advised just to think about it.

Or perhaps it doesn't even bear thinking about.

CHAPTER ELEVEN

Coming To Terms

While you're at it, why not learn some of the commoner words of DIY-speak? You don't actually have to do the jobs or pick up the tools: all you need is to be able to talk about them.

The advantages are several. DIY-speak helps both to comfort and confuse the wife when, in answer to her query about your progress on jobs around the house, you can reply: 'I've just finished chamfering the arris, my love. Next, I'll take a look at the escutcheon on the living room door: check it for blots and all that. After which I shall ensure that there's nothing blocking the hopper head outside the bathroom; check that the garden path is still in situ; level off the made-up ground where necessary, and check that the wainscotting has not exceeded the height of the dado.'

While her head is still resounding to the majesty of the words and she is marvelling at the magnitude of the tasks you have undertaken – which tasks together should take about thirty seconds – you can nip off to the pub. There you can join the other renegade do-it-yourselfers as they stand around and bluff each other with a few choice phrases interspersed with indistinct mutterings:

'Yerss . . I filleted the old flaunchings . . . rhubarb rhubarb . . . checked the old jumper on the kitchen tap . . . rhubarb rhubarb . . . kerfed a few bits of timber . . . rhubarb rhubarb . . . and then decided to take a quick break before I started on the catslide for the lean-to . . .'

All you need do is learn three or four new terms a day, boned up before you leave the house, and you can make your own contribution, secure in the knowledge that those around you haven't done a stroke themselves. Not only that: they may have no idea what you're rabbiting on about, but dare not admit it in case they blow their own cover.

Make sure you go through the whole alphabet to choose your new words. Otherwise you'll be in the position of the man who has just subscribed to a natural history part-work and can tell you everything you ever wanted to know about aardvarks, but doesn't know the first bloody thing about zebras.

ADJUSTABLE WRENCH. A wrench with one fixed and one opening jaw. Sometimes termed a MONKEY GRIP. Careful how you apply pressure: a sudden jerk or slip could put your back out.

Not to be confused with an ADJUSTABLE WENCH, although she, too, could put your back out, especially if she got you in the monkey grip.

AGGREGATE. Material mixed in with cement to make concrete or mortar. Fine aggregate is sand; coarse aggregate is gravel. All-in aggregate is sand and gravel mixed.

All-in aggregate is usually delivered on the eve of a torrential downpour. Next morning, the gravel is still where it was dumped. The washed-out sand is spread all over the garden and has blocked the drains of several houses along the row. You are not very popular.

ARRIS. The sharp edge formed by two surfaces meeting at an angle, such as the corner of a brick or stone. A recessed window set into such a corner is referred to as a pane in the arris.

ARRISSING. Smoothing the edges of newly cut glass with an abrasive stone. Not to be confused with ARRISSING ABOUT, a useful technique for avoiding any actual work.

BAT. A brick cut widthwise for bonding purposes.

Term of abuse employed by DIY men towards a nagging wife or mother-in-law, usually prefixed by 'old', as in: 'Oh, belt up, you old bat.'

BEAM. A timber, concrete or steel lintel used to bridge an opening and support the weight above.

The smile on a DIY man's face as he completes an arduous, boring or tricky job; swiftly wiped off as he realises he's painted himself into a corner or bricked himself in.

BENCHING. The concrete surface inside a manhole. Not to be confused with BELCHING, a condition often brought about by bending double to apply the benching. Nor with WENCHING, which is what 99.9 per cent of the benchers wish they were doing instead. (The remaining 0.1 per cent has slipped a disc. His only immediate wish is for somebody to turn up and get them out of the manhole.)

BITS. Detachable steel cutting tools used in hand or power drills for boring holes in different kinds of materials. They come in a wide range of sizes, as any hospital casualty officer will confirm.

BITUMINOUS FELT. A weatherproof covering for roofing. Often not weatherproof after laying if the DIY ace isn't careful where he puts his big feet.

BLEEDING. Blemishes in paintwork caused by seepage from underneath.

The seepage of vital fluids through the skin of the average do-it-yourselfer after only five minutes on any given job.

The adjective applied to any given job by the bleeding do-it-yourselfer.

BLIND NAILING. A method of nailing down tongue-and-grooved boards so that the nails don't show. Usually given up after five minutes in favour of the more straightforward bash-it-and-bend-it method.

BLISTERING. Bubbles on paintwork caused by the expansion of moisture trapped under the paint.

Bubbles on the skin of the home handyman after 10 seconds under the sink with a blowlamp.

BOILER. Water heater, often part of a central heating system.

Term of endearment, usually prefixed by 'old' (see BAT), applied by the DIY man to the woman in his life.

BOTTLE TRAP. Bottle-shaped fitting under bath or sink.

Any form of completed enclosure (brickwork, panelling, etc.) behind which the DIY enthusiast has left his bottle of whisky. Seems such a shame to pull it down.

BRICKS. Rectangular blocks of burnt clay. Usually of two main types:

(a) Those which are needed whole, but which arrive broken.

(b) Those which need to be broken to end a course, but which won't break in a million years.

Wet bricks are much heavier than dry bricks, a fact which becomes apparent as soon as one lands on your foot.

BRUISING. Indentations in the surface of wood, often caused by hammer blows.

Discoloured indentations on the skin of the amateur builder, often caused by hammer blows. Bruising on the skin of the amateur is a fair indication of his degree of skill: if he finishes a job black and blue from head to foot, he's not very good at it.

BRUSHES. Things with handles at one end and hairs at the other, used in the application of paint, etc. The paint is applied with the hairy end, which helps to give that attractive furry surface. Brushes needed for the next paint job can be found in garages and sheds, stiff and clogged, two years after the last paint job.

BUILDING LINE. A line beyond which a building may not project, which is exceeded by several inches when the man next door builds an extension. Should you complain about this, the local authority may order him to demolish the extension and start again. Upon which he will call round for a man-to-man chat and hit you with a shovel.

BULL NOSE. A term applied to certain bricks and planes because of their rounded corners.

Also applied to do-it-yourselfers who have come into closer contact with their constructions than they intended (see DRILLS).

CARPETS. Natural or man-made fibre floor coverings, of which wool is the most expensive.

Measuring and laying a carpet yourself saves the expense of hiring a skilled man, but this may be offset by the discovery that the roll you ordered is two feet shorter then the room.

Over-ordering is not quite so common, but at least means you can carpet another room or have a few free doormats. If you do not have another room which needs carpeting, or are well-fixed for doormats, you could always build an extension.

CARPET TILES. Squares of carpeting, very easy for the amateur to lay.

Any under-ordering can be resolved by going back to the supplier, who tells you ever so gently that the line has been discontinued.

Should you over-order and take back the two dozen spares, the man shrugs sadly and asks, 'Who wants 'em in that colour these days?'

CATSLIDE ROOF. A roof which sweeps down from the main structure almost to ground level. The best kind of roof to fall off.

CEMENT. A material that sets hard when mixed with water. Its rapid setting qualities are demonstrated when a load of ready-mixed arrives last thing at night or when you are out for the day.

CESSPOOL or CESSPIT. An underground chamber used for the storage of domestic sewage. It is usually emptied regularly, often for a fee, by local authorities. Emptying a cesspit yourself is not recommended. Even if you don't fall in, you feel very lonely for days afterwards.

CHISELS. Wood chisels are sharp tools for shaping wood, paring ends off thumbs or making holes in kneecaps. Metal or masonry chisels are not so sharp, but are much bigger and heavier. While they don't penetrate as far into thumbs, kneecaps, etc., they make up for it by making a bigger mess of the surface area.

CHUCK. The part of a drill which holds the bit.

What many amateurs do with a job when the first flush of enthusiasm wears off, then used as 'chuck it'.

CISTERN. Cold water storage tank with an open top, situated in the loft. The open top is best covered. Otherwise it makes a tidy receptacle for bits of mortar, broken tiles, dead mice, birds and disorientated bats.

CLOUT. A short, galvanised nail with a large, flat head.

The chastisement meted out by a harassed do-it-yourselfer to his bothersome young son. Usually inflicted on his tiny, pointed head.

CONTACT ADHESIVE. Adhesive which is allowed almost to dry before the surfaces are brought together, upon which they bond instantly. At which point the do-it-yourselfer notices that one bit is sticking out further than the other. And that the bit that is sticking out is glued firmly to his finger.

CRAMPS. Tools with a screw mechanism used to hold materials together while glueing.

What the DIY man gets after fiddling under the sink for half an hour.

CRAZY PAVING. Broken slabs of stone or concrete laid down to form a paved surface. Often delivered as whole slabs, but accidents will happen.

DADO. For some strange and doubtless Freudian reason, sounds vaguely disgusting. Simply means the lower half of a wall, covered in wood panelling or embossed paper. Which comes as a disappointment to everybody.

DOORS. The things you unscrew from their hinges and lean against the wall for a couple of years.

DRAIN RODS. A set of cane rods, used for clearing drains. Can be hired from builders merchants, who, for a small extra charge, will call round and retrieve the rods after you've got them stuck in the drain.

DRILLS. Things for boring holes in things.

A BREAST DRILL is a hand drill which incorporates a curved broad plate, against which the user can lean to increase pressure while drilling. When the bit hits a cavity, or goes suddenly through the other side, the user gets a bonus of a second hole which appears higher up the wall, though it doesn't do his nose much good (see BULL NOSE).

The term HAND DRILL is a misnomer. When the thing slips, it usually drills your knee.

The POWER DRILL makes a lot of noise, but makes the user feel really professional. Best avoided for psychological reasons if you have a dental appointment pending, and best switched off for physical reasons before being used to scratch the head.

ESCUTCHEON. The plate that surrounds a keyhole. Usually blotted when you paint the door.

FLASHING. A strip of lead, zinc, copper or bituminous felt, used to waterproof external junctions in buildings.

A form of anti-social behaviour uncommon among do-it-yourselfers, if only because they don't have the strength left for it.

FLEXIBLE RULE. A spring-loaded tape coiled in a casing. When the end is released after use, the tape whizzes back clear inside the case. It can be recovered quite easily with a bit of wire in only a few hours.

GLASS. Transparent silicate which can be cut to any desired shape, using a glass cutter, styptic pencil and home first aid kit.

GLASS CUTTER. A tool for cutting glass, often with a hardened steel wheel. Some types have replaceable wheels. Scientists are working on a formula for replaceable fingers.

GROUND. A piece of wood used to fix skirting boards to walls.

The top bit of the Earth's surface which prevents a do-it-yourselfer falling 40 feet from a 30-foot ladder.

HOPPER HEAD. A funnel-shaped fitting on a drainpipe.

A term of endearment applied by his Ever-Loving to the bungling DIY man, along with similar epithets such as Numbskull, Lamebrain, and Idiot Features.

IN SITU. Latin for 'in place'. Used to describe concrete laid where it is intended to stay when dry, or for paving slabs laid in position.

The one place the wife disapproves of. When the drying time is up, she decides she would like the path over there.

LAGGING. Strips of felt or tubes of foam rubber used to insulate water pipes.

LAGGING BEHIND is what the DIY man does on a job, usually after his energy starts flagging. This is often cured by nagging.

JUMPER. Part of a water tap to which the washer is attached.

Article of clothing which the DIY man gets covered in paint. It always turns out to be his best one.

JUNIOR HACKSAW. Small saw used for fine metal jobs. Often borrowed by younger members of the family for their own DIY experiments, such as sawing the legs off the plant stand which took Dad three months to make.

KERFING. Parallel, half-depth saw cuts made in wood to enable it to be curved. Not to be confused with KOFFING, which is caused by heavy breathing in a cloud of sawdust.

LINTEL. Short beam across a door or window, against which the head is banged at regular intervals during painting jobs.

LOFT LADDER. Retractable ladder fitted to a trap door leading into the loft. Safer than an ordinary ladder because nobody can take it away while you're working.

MADE-UP GROUND. Ground built up to new levels or excavations filled in with earth. Erections built on made-up ground are those that have sunk.

MAKE GOOD. Repairing damage or improving on bad workmanship. Professional craftsmen get much of their living from making good the efforts of amateur DIY men.

MALLET. Wooden hammer used where a metal hammer might damage the object being struck, such as a chisel handle or the left thumb.

MATT FINISH. A dull finish to paint or varnish. Mostly intentional, but it can be accidental, such as when the cat has got stuck to the wet paint or the kids have rubbed it down with a duster. (The paint, not the cat, though it is not unknown for the kids to rub down wet paint with the cat. The cat is seldom amused.)

MIXER VALVE. A control valve which mixes hot and cold water to provide a supply in a shower which boils you alive or brings you out in icicles.

NON-DRIP PAINT. What it says. It doesn't drip. The fact that the painter is covered in it within half an hour suggests that it creeps.
NON-LOAD BEARING WALL. The wall standing next to the load-bearing wall you've just knocked down.
NON-CONCUSSIVE TAP. The tap you don't bang your head on.

OFF-CUTS. The bits left over after joints or shapes have been cut in wood. Best not thrown away: you'll need some of them to make good the lengths you've cut short, or the joints you've got back-to-front.

Many DIY enthusiasts keep off-cuts in a bag for possible future use. The bag clutters up the garage for a couple of years and is finally thrown away. Next day, along comes a job for which off-cuts would have been ideal.
OPEN PLAN. Design of a house so that it has few interior walls, giving an effect of spaciousness. Enables the whole family to share in the delights of television, video games, record players, squabbling kids and fighting pets. Some people prefer the old-fashioned claustrophobia.
OPEN RISER. Staircase with treads but no risers. (Staircases with risers but no treads have never caught on.) Allows the light to reach areas underneath the staircase, which is very useful for rescuing the kids when they've slipped through the spaces where the risers should have been.
OVERFLOW. A pipe leading from a cistern and protruding beyond an outer wall. It prevents internal flooding by causing external flooding instead, and also acts as a warning. On hearing the

first sounds of splashing, go outside and stand under the pipe for a few seconds. If you return soaking wet, it's either raining buckets or you have an overflow.

PARTING SLIP. Strip of wood in a sash window which separates the weights. Sometimes known as a WAGTAIL.

Also the last action of a DIY man on a ladder or a scaffolding frame, often caused by his stepping back to admire his work. After which he is seldom known as a wagtail.

PARTY WALL. The wall dividing two terraced or semi-detached houses, occasionally knocked down in a fit of enthusiasm. The wall is usually owned jointly, so you could always ask the man next door to contribute half the cost of rebuilding it. His answer is fairly predictable.

QUOIN. The outer corner of a building, set at a right angle.

A SQUINT QUOIN is the outer corner of a building or wall which is either more or less than a right angle.

Useful to remember, that. If someone comments on your quoins not being exactly true, you can reply immediately with, 'Of course not. Thought it needed a few squint quoins here and there.' That should shut him up.

READY-MIXED CONCRETE. Freshly mixed concrete delivered by lorry. Cuts out a lot of the labour and is easily handled, providing the site has been prepared properly and that there are enough helpers to get the job done quickly.

What happens in practice is that the delivery is late, the helpers have gone home, it's raining cats and dogs and it's getting dark. That wouldn't be so bad if you hadn't forgotten to board off the end of the site.

RELIEF WALLPAPER. Wallpaper with a raised pattern with which you cover up your attempts at plastering. So called because when the wife sees the result, she says, 'That's a relief.'

RULES. Measuring instruments, of which most modern ones are made with imperial measures on one side and metric on the other. With either, you always start at the wrong end.

A FOLDING RULE, useful for working in confined spaces, is pivoted and hinged to fold down to a quarter of its length. This often has to be done with one hand, and really skilled DIY men have been known to do it without trapping their fingers. If you can roll a cigarette with one hand while standing on your head on horseback, you can work underneath a sink with a folding rule.

With a ZIGZAG rule – pivoted every 6½ inches of its 6-foot-6-inch length – you're really in trouble.

SCAFFOLDING TOWER. Easily-erected sectional tower which provides a safe platform from which to do high jobs. It is sometimes fitted with wheels, which makes for a less safe platform when erected on a sloping path. Failure to secure it can mean, at best, that you finish up painting the house next door; at worst, that you're picked up for speeding on the motorway.

SEMI-PLAIN WALLPAPER does not have to be matched. (Yes, there are papers that *do* have to be matched. Sorry about that.)

SHAKES. Splits in timber caused by seasoning.

Shakes can also afflict the do-it-yourselfer, usually halfway through a job; often caused by the realisation that while he's sweating himself into an early grave, everybody else is down at the pub.

SHOOTING. Planing the edge of the board.

Not to be confused with SHOOTING A LINE, which is what you do in the pub afterwards (see SHAKES).

SHORING. Temporary support to a structure which is being altered, for example, the bit of wood you accidentally kick from under the concrete windowsill, which then falls down and alters your foot.

Not to be confused with SNORING, which is a dead giveaway when you're supposed to be working in the shed.

SPIRIT LEVEL. A tool containing one or more curved transparent tubes filled with alcohol, chloroform or oil. Each tube contains a bubble of air, which rises to the highest point to register 'level' when held horizontally.

Some of the cheaper models will register level when laid on a ski slope. All you can do then, unless you're laying a ski slope, is break open the tube and hope it contains a stiff dose of alcohol or chloroform.

STABLE DOOR. Two-part door, hung so that the top half can be open while the bottom one remains closed. Useful for containing children or animals until they've worked it out. No use closing it after children or horses have bolted, unless you'd rather not have them back.

STOPCOCK. A tap which controls the water supply to a house. There are usually two: one outside and one inside. In the event of a burst, the outside one can seldom be found, usually because you concreted it over when you resurfaced the path. If you do find it, you can't locate the key which turns it.

The inside one may be discovered somewhere under the sink unit, behind the catfood and detergents. This is the one which is always stuck, but one turn of the monkey wrench usually brings results – the head of the tap breaks off. At this point you turn to the Yellow Pages.

STRUCTURAL WALL. A load-bearing wall, often difficult for the amateur to distinguish from a non-load bearing wall. You can tell the difference as soon as you've knocked it down, from the way the ceiling and a double bed fall on your head.

STRUTTING. Timber used in a roof frame as a strengthener. Also what the DIY man indulges in as soon as he's finished a job. Best not to strut too far if you're working on the roof. (See PARTING SLIP.)

VICE. Device for holding materials firm for sawing, etc.

An enjoyable but often anti-social occupation such as gambling, boozing or womanising, which the do-it-yourselfer keeps promising himself he'll take up one day. Should he live so long.

WAINSCOT. Wood panelling on a wall up to dado height. If you've got panelling up to your dado, you'll know it's a wainscot.

WALL FIXING. The different kinds of proprietary fittings such as wall plugs, toggles, anchor bolts, etc., which never fall out or work loose when the man next door fixes them.

WATER HAMMER. Loud noise and vibration in pipework when the tap is turned on. Can be cured by repacking the gland nut on the top, fitting an air chamber to the ball valve, or stuffing your ears with cotton wool.

CHAPTER TWELVE

Mind Your Language

Do-it-yourself language has a poetry all its own. The original version of Kipling's *If*, quoted in Chapter Four, is but one of the treasures of our literary heritage inspired by the honest toil of home maintenance.

There are others? Of course there are others: not just in poetry, but also in song. Here are four original versions of songs which have since become classics. The later versions of these became cheapened and diluted by the alteration of the words to appeal to a wider market. But today, with the worldwide increase in DIY, the originals are coming back into their own.

The comments preceding each song should help to put the situations and sentiments into their sociological context. Readers of a sensitive, nervous or aesthetic disposition are warned that certain aspects of the lyrics may be disturbing or cause offence. But what the hell.

There is a certain return to the primitive brought out by the sheer muckiness of DIY operations, a messing about in mud, dust, sand and plaster that brings out the scruffy little boy in every man. At weekends he can defy convention: neglect to shave, neglect even to wash. What's the point if he'll be covered in grime within five minutes?

The regression can go too far, however, and bring out scruffy-little-boy traits that his mother would never stand for and his wife certainly won't. Wiping his nose on the sleeve, for instance, intense and perverse pleasure that it is, has to stop once he's been caught at it:

Green sleeves were all my joy-oy,
And oh, green sleeves were my delight.
'Til the wife made me use a hankie
And took all the shine off my green sleeves . . .

The primitive comes out, too, with the immense physical exertion of the heavier jobs. This can lead to the handyman going at it hell-for-leather, overtaxing both his expertise and his strength and doing himself a mischief. As witness this song, the inspiration for the later *Volga Boatman*:

Barrow half-filled.
GRUNT!
I'm daft and half-skilled.
GRUNT!
Back's cracked,
I'm whacked,
More than half-killed.
AAARGH!

The real enthusiast can reach a pitch of fervour which begins to worry those around him. With a fanatical gleam in his eye, he rushes around bashing and banging at everything in sight, and sometimes – for his own good – he has to be taken off the job.

Not that he goes without a fight. As he's dragged off before he knocks the whole house down, he can be heard singing, to the tune that became *Rule Britannia*:

Rule, Dee Eye Why!
Dee Eye Why's all the rage!
That's why
I am being put back
In
My
Cage . . .

The everyday terms, the very words, used in DIY have a genuinely poetic ring about them, a harking back to a more colourful and elegant age. Consider the richness of this old Austrian DIY song, the inspiration for the later *My Favourite Things*:

Cavity infills
And filleted flaunchings,
Capillaries jointed
And shellac on knottings.

Rivets ball-peined,
S-traps well drained.
All it needs now is a fence post well strained . . .

Ballcocks and draincocks,
Balusters and noggings,
Timber on dados,
And grout in the hoggings.
Barbels, perpends,
Epoxy resins.
These are just some of my favourite things . . .

The richness of the language makes DIY-speak ideal for cursing. The curses, what's more, can be used within shot of the most sensitive ears. All they do is *sound* obscene: there's nothing about the actual words to which anybody could take exception, unless you're into such specialities as bastard wood rasps.

So you can let off steam, when you've accidentally bashed your thumb or sawn your leg off, with such resounding expletives as:

Ballcocks!
Ball-peins!
Balusters!
Capillaries!
Cesspits!
Draincocks!
Epoxies!
Shellacs!
Weep holes!

There are also phrases appropriate to cursing, all of them genuine DIY terms:

Anaglypta me dados!

Angle me arris!
Anodise me oxides!
Backfill me footings!
Ball-pein me rivets!
Baluster me banisters!
Bevel me battens!
Blister me blockboards!
Bracket me risers!
Carborundum me oilstones!
Chamfer me arris!
Corbel me roof truss!
Draw off me dead leg!
Edge me wagtail!
Fillet me flaunching!
Nail me noggings!
Open me draincock!
Plaster me perpends!
Shellac me knottings!

The DIY cuss-words and phrases can be used to great effect in Christmas pantos and amateur productions of *Treasure Island*.

(Enter Long John Silver, crutch a-clump and parrot askew, roaring: 'Timber me dados and draw off me dead leg! I'll have yer flaunchings filleted, Jim 'Awkins! Corbel me roof trusses if I don't!')

(Exit stage left, muttering, 'Plaster me perpends and shellac me knottings! Them as dies'll be the lucky ones . . .')

They are a great help, too, to the non-DIY man forced into the company of enthusiasts in a pub. By swearing lustily he can establish himself as a macho Jack-the-Lad, and at the same time give the impression of being totally immersed in DIY:

'Well, chamfer me arris, if it isn't old Fred! Blistering blockboards, it's weeks since I've seen you. Infill me cavities and anodise me oxides if I'm not going to buy you a pint, you old bastard rasp!'

Realising you have knowledge so encyclopaedic that it has affected even your speech patterns, everybody around looks at you in awe and hangs on your every word. You are established as the DIY expert of the saloon bar, which gets embarrassing because you are asked for advice every five minutes.

Cope with the pestering by dishing out vague but confident wisdom. 'Three of sand, one of cement. Never fails.' 'Prime it and seal it.' 'Start as you mean to carry on.'

The other possible reaction is that everybody considers you to be a boring old fart and moves away. At least then you won't have to buy any more pints for old bastard rasps.

CHAPTER THIRTEEN

Make It Or Break It: It's All In The Stars

Ready, willing and able as you are; keen as mustard and ever-eager to demonstrate your skills as a handyman, there may be a factor in your makeup which leaves the finished result a little short of perfection. The factor need be nothing big: simply a small flaw such as total ineptitude, lack of co-ordination, or a proneness to disaster against which the *Titanic* appears an A1 insurance risk.

You can anticipate the results of your efforts by reading your stars through your zodiacal sign. Gemini, for instance, never finishes anything he undertakes. Libra and Pisces, both bone idle, often have more sense than to start. Sagittarius, big though he thinks, is far too scruffy and impatient with detail to produce anything which looks good or won't fall down within 10 minutes.

Cancer is keen but clumsy, and often finishes a job with a bit of his person missing. Aries often finishes with lots of bits missing.

Then there's kindly, dreamy Aquarius, who spends so much time helping others – often Leo, the archetypal bossyboots – that he never gets anything done himself.

Those who do get things done are Taurus, with a head-down, determined approach; Scorpio, who bashes everything into submission; steady plodder Capricorn, and pain-in-the-bum perfectionist Virgo.

Should you be unfortunate enough to belong to one of these last four signs, all is not lost. You can always excuse any lack of skill, enthusiasm or interest by claiming that you have Libra rising, Sagittarius sinking, or Pisces going round in circles.

ARIES (March 21 – April 20)

Dynamic. Bursting with energy. Full of ideas. Self-assured. Keen to be first in everything.

That's Aries, first sign of the Zodiac, ruled by Mars and ready to tackle any problem, no matter how big. Ideal for a do-it-yourselfer, wouldn't you think?

The answer is no. Never in a million years. And if you are among his Nearest and Dearest, you'd be well advised to dissuade him from any DIY activity. Otherwise you'll find that you're doing his do-it-yourself yourself.

Airies is a born leader and practises two of the great arts of leadership: Inspiration and Delegation.

Inspiration means getting people worked up about a project and irrevocably committed to it. Delegation means clearing off and letting them get on with it.

Aries will often get involved in DIY because he believes that nobody else can do anything as well as he. What's the sense in paying a professional when he – Aries – can do a much superior job in less time and for half the money?

The sense becomes apparent after he's unscrewed the doors, soaked a bit of paper off the dining room ceiling, drilled a few dozen holes here and there, burned off a few square inches of paint and knocked a couple of bricks out of a connecting wall.

That's his bit over with. He's started. Shown the way. Now the rest of you can carry on. Any questions? Good.

Aries' ideas and energy are paralleled by a chronic lack of patience and total inattention to detail. OK, that replacement pane of glass *is* half an inch short all round. How was he to know you had to measure right up to the frame and not just up to the putty? And OK, he *has* knocked out the old pane. And OK, the blizzard *is* whistling through the living room. And OK, it *is* Christmas and there's not a shop open for days. Is he supposed to think of *everything*?

As the baby of the Zodiac, he's vulnerable to criticism. Can't take it. Easily hurt. When it's tactfully suggested that perhaps he shouldn't have had the ready-mixed cement dropped before he laid the hardcore and fixed the framing for the path, his reactions are not exactly adult. Not unless adult behaviour includes losing your temper and bawling at everything in sight.

Another reason for keeping Aries away from jobs around the house is that he's the most accident-prone sign of the Zodiac. The head and face are the prime areas, followed closely by the kneecaps.

When Aries is working in a confined space, damage to the face could be done by those very kneecaps, and that damage to the kneecaps could be done by that very face. The British Medical Association is rumoured to be locked in a demarcation dispute with the British Dental Association about who pulls teeth from lacerated kneecaps.

Brave as he is in many ways, Aries cannot stand pain. When his teeth meet his knees, or his knees meet his teeth, he reacts like a child, yelling blue murder until somebody slaps a few plasters on or kisses it better.

Like a child, he soon forgets the pain and laughs at the fuss he made. 'My, my,' he says, 'I wonder how I came to have a silly accident like that.'

As an aid to concentration, he scratches his head with an electric drill which he's forgotten to switch off.

Inattention to detail, you see. That's what it's usually put down to at the inquest.

TAURUS (April 21 – May 20)

Taurus takes his time, does a job steadily, and does it well. He plans out a job to the last detail, but without fuss. He moves into it quietly, and tidies up before he moves out.

Always ready with help and advice, he's a good man to live next door to. Or he would be, if your own tatty efforts weren't always compared with his.

He's a man of few words. Sometimes too few, as in the story of the Taurean who was fixing some roof timbers when an agitated neighbour rushed round and shouted, 'Hey! Your house is on fire!'

'I know,' said Taurus.

'Aren't you going to jump?'

'No.'

'Aren't you going to climb down the drainpipe, then?'

'No.'

'Aren't you even going to move to the other side of the roof before the smoke gets to you?'

'No.'

'For God's sake, man! Why not?'

'My foot's stuck.'

Taureans of both sexes like security, and their penchant for DIY is part of the reassurance that their house is as good as they can make it. The garden is a model of ordered colour, though never in a regimented or fussy way. And the house is usually full of flowers, properly arranged and not just dumped in the nearest milk bottle.

Work around the house is the Taurus way of relaxing. Even the preferred TV programmes are those on practical or creative subjects such as pottery, painting or flower arranging.

Nor is the garden just for show. Taurus grows most of the family's vegetables and probably runs a few chickens, possibly even a goat. When neighbours ask, 'What about the smell?', the practical Taurus reply is, 'The goat will just have to get used to it.'

Strong as the bull of his sign, Taurus moves easily through the heaviest jobs. The sign tends to run to fat though, and the excess pounds can sometimes lead to embarrassments such as having to be hauled out bodily by the fire brigade from a cramped position under the sink.

Among Taurus' weak spots are the back and the legs. He should take special care when he's lifting anything heavy, if he doesn't want to risk being carted off bent double in a wheelbarrow. Gout is one of the problems, too, so it behoves him not to drop too many bricks.

The throat is another vulnerable area, and Taurus should beware of working in dusty, unventilated spaces: a coughing fit could result in his weak back slipping a disc. By this time the fire brigade could be getting a bit fed up of prising the same overweight DIY enthusiast from under the same sink, although it gives the gallant lads something to talk about when they get home after a hard day's fire fighting.

'Anything exciting happen today, dear?'

'Not a lot. Cat up a tree. Smithers under the sink again.'

'Really? How's he getting on with his plumbing jobs?'

'Not too badly. Next Sunday he's replacing the waste trap.'

'That's nice, dear. Something to look forward to.'

'Yerss . . . Passes the time, I suppose. Remind me to indent for two heavy duty crowbars and a drum of axle grease, will you, love . . . ?'

GEMINI (May 21 – June 20)

You're slim and agile, always on the go. Boredom is your greatest enemy: you need something happening all the time, the constant challenge of something new.

You are versatile, multi-talented, manually very skilled and can turn your hand to anything. Your mind is analytical, rational, cool, and you make it up quickly. You can do several things at once, effortlessly and always at top speed.

So why does nothing get done?

It's your dual personality that's the trouble. Although you make up your mind quickly, you unmake it just as quickly. Your moods change, too. Yesterday's enthusiasm is today's long yawn. You're

easily bored and skip from one project to another.

If preparation work is boring, you'll start a job in the middle. Or if a job gets finicky halfway through, that's where you'll finish it. And although you are capable of doing several things at once, you are also capable of not doing several things at once.

Skilled though you are, you are not above faking or botching: if you think you can get away with it, you'll try it.

Punctuality has never been your strong point. If you're asked to make sure a job is finished before the in-laws arrive at 4 p.m. on Sunday, you'll start the job at 3.55. Nothing personal: you'd have started then even if you liked the in-laws.

You are best working on your own, mainly because you're easily distracted, but also because you don't like advice or criticism. Especially when you're faking or botching or when the in-laws are standing there covered in plaster dust.

Plaster dust – or any kind of dust – is likely to put a stop to the job anyway. Your weak spot is your lungs, and there's no excuse like a good coughing fit for stopping work.

Despite working best on your own, you are essentially sociable and gregarious and a great talker. So you take your coughing fit down to the pub where you wash the plaster dust from your throat and tell everyone within earshot about the half-dozen jobs you're coping with all at once. You won't tell them that you've been coping with most of them for several months. Nor that, as you left the house, your Ever-Loving was thumbing frantically through the Yellow Pages.

CANCER (June 21 – July 21)

Security is the key to your personality, and your home and garden offer this: retreats from the cold, hard and fearsome world outside.

Money, too, offers protection, so to save on costs you'll do most of the jobs around the house yourself. You're a great hoarder and never throw anything away. Your garage, shed and attic are crammed with bits of things that might come in useful one of these days.

You're generally a bit on the big side, awkward and clumsy in your movements, which makes the accumulated clutter a health hazard. You spend a lot of time falling over it, and it spends a lot of time falling down on you as you stumble through the shed looking for those bits of four-by-two you put away five years ago.

Once you've found all the bits, however, and got your act together, nothing stops you until the job's finished. Although you don't bask in the spotlight like the extrovert Leos or clownish Sagittarians, you do like to be appreciated: a few words of praise do a lot for your undernourished ego. Conversely, you're easily hurt, even by a look of disapproval or a tone of voice that's less than enthusiastic about your efforts.

You tend to brood over mistakes. When your home-built bookcase collapses as soon as somebody puts a book on it, you creep back into your shell and sulk instead of getting out the tools and bashing the bookcase back together again.

Your fondness for water means that one of your early garden projects will probably be a pond. Your natural clumsiness means that you fall into it as soon as it's filled.

Part of your defence against reality is a love of the past, a yearning for the good old days, and this reflects itself in your home and garden. Your furniture is period, reproduction or home-made: solid stuff that lasts a lifetime and stands up well to your habit of falling over it. Your garden is planted with the tried-and-trusted old-fashioned varieties: not as showy as the modern strains, but guaranteed to grow and bloom despite the fuss and attention you lavish on them.

Your vulnerable areas are the chest, knees, kidneys, bladder and skin. You rarely tan, and your skin burns easily in the sun. So be careful when you work outdoors: on a cold day you could finish up with a chill on the kidneys, on a hot day with a severe dose of sunburn. There you are with two of the finest excuses for not doing a stroke outdoors, and all you do is sit indoors and fret, praying for the weather to change so that you can get cracking again.

You do a lot of fretting: self-confidence is not one of your strong points. Except, that is, at the full moon. Then your mood can change rapidly and you're likely to knock down half the house or paint the bedroom a startling shade of pink.

As the moon wanes, however, and probably after a few harsh words from your Nearest and Dearest, you come back to normality. Don't worry: you've got the rest of the month to rebuild the walls and repaint the bedroom.

LEO (July 22 – August 21)

The phrase 'do-it-yourself' is constantly on Leo's lips. He has the bricks delivered, mixes a bit of mortar, then hands the trowel to the nearest member of the family and says, 'There you are – do it yourself.'

Leo is born to lead, a natural boss. He thinks big, acts big, organises everything, and then gets other people to do the work. Nobody's safe. Family, friends, postmen, milkmen, paper boys, Jehovah's Witnesses and passing tramps: they all get roped in if they don't move fast enough.

He has a natural authority and stately bearing that makes others mentally jump to attention when he barks out orders. He bullies, domineers, rants, raves, bellows and chivvies. And everybody loves him for it.

Like the big cats, Leo is capable of spurts of ferocious energy, followed by bouts of comatose lethargy. When he's got everybody fetching, carrying, hammering and sawing, he retreats indoors to recharge his batteries with a couple of snifters and a snooze.

He'll be awake again just as the job is being finished, shower everyone with praise, dish out free advice on what to do about slipped discs and pulled fetlocks, fill everyone up with food and drink, and send them away deeply indebted to him. What they're indebted for, they can't for the life of them remember, but when the aches have subsided and the swellings gone down, they'll all come back for another go.

Leo is never stingy with advice. You can have as much of that as you like; certainly you'll get more than you'll ever need. He won't stop there, either. Having organised his own labour gangs, Leo wanders nextdoor where his neighbour is proudly surveying the brick honeycomb screen he's just built.

'Splendid job, old man,' says Leo. 'Does you proud. Just one thing, though: this brick at the bottom looks a bit on the skew. If I were you, I'd just take it out like – whoops!'

Neatly dodging the crashing bricks, which is more than his neighbour manages, he says, 'Sorry about that, old chap. But I'm sure it won't take you long to build it up again: I'll send some people round to help if you like. Get the bottom courses dead straight: that's the secret. Oh, and I'd put some butter on that bump on your head if I were you.'

One way of getting Leo to do anything himself is to flatter him. Once he's been assured that he's the greatest artist and craftsman since Leonardo, he'll roll up his sleeves, pick up the trowel and get to work. Not for long, though: if one disaster doesn't overtake him, another will.

He's accident prone, for a start: vulnerable in the spine and generative organs, and prone to hoarseness and sore throats. So if he doesn't put his back out or do a nasty to his naughty bits on a barrow handle, he's liable to go down with a bad attack of the wheezes. His heart could act up a bit as well, especially since his lifestyle tends more to over-indulgence than regular exercise.

All in all, it's best to let him give the orders and get on with the job yourself. When it's over, you'll love him for it. It says here.

VIRGO (August 22 – September 21)

Virgo is neat, clean, fastidious, industrious, hardworking, methodical, a chronic worrier and a fanatic for order. Virgo, in short, is a pain in the bum.

There, there. Only kidding. Joke. Ha ha. But nobody comes out well from comparison with a Virgo. Unless it's Capricorn, who's almost as big a pain.

Virgo is always thinking of the family: how to please them, how to make life more comfortable. So he or she will make life more comfortable for them whether they want it or not, and regardless of how much discomfort they have to endure while the work's going on.

And it *will* go on. Virgo is a perfectionist, and does everything the hard way. There's never any skimping or botching. And if the finished job isn't perfect in every detail, it may well get done all over again. If the colour isn't dead right in a newly painted room, Virgo will repaint the whole room and think nothing of it. The occupant of the room doesn't think much of it, either.

Modesty is another of Virgo's attributes. A lady Virgoan will show somebody round the house she's decorated from top to bottom, then proudly point to the comatose form on the settee and say, 'Of course, I couldn't have done it without my husband. He put the ladders away.'

Mind you, Virgo might as well be occupied with DIY. There is a tendency towards knock knees, bow legs, a big head, a squashed or unshapely nose, often one shoulder lower than the other. And

that's *before* they start. With all that going for them, they're better off doing something useful indoors than roaming the streets and frightening the horses.

And being busy helps to stop the fretting. Virgo is a chronic worrier. So if he or she asks your opinion on the colour of the newly painted ceiling, say it's great. Magic. Just right. Couldn't be better. Praise it any less, and Virgo won't sleep a wink that night – worse, will probably get up in the small hours and start all over again.

Although Virgo is constantly on the go, there's never a trail of dust and debris through the house, as in the homes of some we could mention. Virgo can't stand dirt or mess, and cleans up as the job progresses.

The sign is that of the archetypal hypochondriac – and well it may be, with weak spots in the head, stomach, feet, hips, arms and shoulders, and a tendency towards gout, rheumatism, backache and liver trouble. So Virgo always has a well-stocked medicine chest and first aid kit.

Because of the sign's careful working habits, however, the first aid kit is seldom used. It's called for mainly to patch up the Aries and Sagittarius who call round to borrow a screwdriver and slip on the mat in the highly polished hall.

Virgo is not known as a pain in the bum for nothing.

LIBRA (September 22 – October 22)

Libra is the sign of marriage and partnership. What this means in practical do-it-yourself terms is that the Libra man lets his wife do it. The Libran's home often reflects the partner's tastes. Which, as he's let the wife do it, comes as no surprise.

The Libran's partner has to make almost all the decisions. Libra is the sign of the scales. Though now and again they're in balance, they spend most of the time swinging up and down, and Libra can't even make up his mind whether or not he's indecisive.

Not only is Libra indecisive, he's also bone idle and easily bored. Add to that the fact that his constitution is delicate – that is, any kind of exertion brings on the vapours – and you don't have the makings of a DIY fanatic.

The indecision doesn't stop him handing out free advice. If there's anything he's good at, it's telling others how to get on with the job. But it does mean that the advice is never the same for two days running.

After telling his partner that the only colour for the living room is apple green, he wanders downstairs next morning, gazes around the half-painted room, and announces that if he were doing the job he'd have chosen cream.

This very indecision can affect his health, as he is hit smartly over the head with a half-empty tin of apple green paint. 'Thank God it was half empty,' he thinks as he crumples at the knees. 'Or was it half full . . . ?'

To be fair, Libra *can* work quite happily for short bursts. But, with the lowest endurance level in the Zodiac, he's ready to give up on the slightest pretext. Nor is he too proud to admit failure: his motto is that if at first you don't succeed, pack it in.

A sense of beauty and harmony is an intrinsic part of the Libran nature. So he's never short of ideas for improving the home. But that's where he prefers his contribution to stop: before he has to roll his sleeves up.

He can't work in dirt or mess, and he puts off any kind of unsavoury job as long as possible. He'll ignore a blocked drain until the thing is overflowing all over the yard. The first prod of the drain rods brings on another attack of the vapours, and it's left to the partner or a helpful neighbour to finish the job. Meanwhile, Libra nips indoors to tidy himself up.

One of Libra's characteristics is the well-bred, cool, unruffled look. At the end of a day's project, he stands there without a hair out of place, without a crease in his shirt, without the tiniest bead of sweat on his brow. The answer is not far to seek: just look for the partner or neighbour standing there exhausted, bedraggled and ready to drop.

Typically Libra was the husband who was found by a friend sitting in a garden chair and drinking beer from a can. At the far end of the garden, his wife was struggling with a wheelbarrow full of rockery stones.

'I can see your wife's working hard,' said the friend. 'But what's the matter with you? Put your back out or something?'

'No,' said the husband. 'It's the wife I'm doing this for. I want to make sure that if anything happens to me she'll be able to cope on her own.'

SCORPIO
(October 23 – November 21)

There are three ways of doing things: the Right Way, the Wrong Way, the Scorpio Way. Scorpio would prefer you to do things his way. Otherwise he may be compelled, reluctantly, to hit you with a brick.

The most forceful personality of the Zodiac, Scorpio is physically very powerful, whether he's wiry and slim or weighty and solid. He's very serious at everything he attempts, and the way he takes things to extremes frightens the life out of even the extremists.

If Scorpio lays a concrete path, it's 18 inches thick – that's just the concrete; the hardcore could build a dam – and wouldn't look out of place on the Maginot Line. His garden pond could take the *Titanic* without overflowing and still leave room for the iceberg.

He lays his plans very thoroughly, reading the DIY guides from cover to cover. Waste of time, really, because he'll do it his way in the end, and he's never wrong. Just ask him. OK, so he has put his new front door on upside down. Looks better like that. It's not your front door, anyway. What the hell's it got to do with you?

That extension he's built: it doesn't cross over the boundary line into your ground next door, does it? Of course if doesn't, Stupid. You must have moved the boundary when he wasn't looking. And what do surveyors know, anyway?

He's very competitive and doesn't believe in just keeping up with the Joneses. He makes the Joneses look the poverty-stricken peasants they are. If the Joneses build a toolshed, he builds a ranch-style summer house with overhanging eaves and a fenced-off porch. If the Joneses put in a modest fishpond, he produces an enormous rock-built job with a couple of waterfalls and a fountain. The Joneses stick up a rustic bird table, he builds a concrete Gothic folly.

Had enough, Jones? Don't start thinking of building a conservatory or you'll find a two-storey brick extension blocking your light.

You can't escape from Scorpio by creeping off to the pub for a quiet pint. He buttonholes you there to talk do-it-yourself. *His* do-it-yourself: who the hell's interested in yours? Here, look at these plans for the new garage. And these photographs of the work so far. Pretty damn good, eh?

If you value your front teeth, they're pretty damn good.

Scorpio doesn't mince words. You've probably noticed. Don't

ask his opinion of your latest effort if you're not prepared to have it criticised.

'*Your* new garage? Don't reckon it'll stand up more than six months. You got those footings all wrong for a start. And you call that bricklaying? I've seen Spanish pigsties built better than that. And why did you pick that timber for the beams? A couple of rainy spells and you'll have a roof like a switchback. Best thing you can do is pull the lot down and start again. And this time, do it *properly* . . .'

Scorpio is the most highly sexed of the zodiacal signs, and his bedroom decor reflects this. He'll spend any amount of money on the means to the end: concealed lighting, enormous bed, mirrors on the ceiling. The best you can hope for is that one night he falls off the chandelier.

SAGITTARIUS
(November 22 – December 20)

Sagittarius is strong, lively, restless, enthusiastic, artistic, quick in his movements and constantly in search of a challenge. With all that going for him, how come his place is in such a mess?

The supreme optimist, he cheerfully promises what he hasn't a hope in hell of delivering. He's quick to grasp a scheme, wants instant results, and throws himself into a job without another thought. When the time does come for thought – when it's time to get down to the finicky but important details – he loses interest. That job will wait, half finished, in a long line of other half finished jobs. Meanwhile, Sagittarius is rushing out with pick, spade and supreme confidence to start another one.

The inside of his house is as big a mess as the outside. He has no patience at all with little jobs. The cupboard door's hanging off? Not to worry: just be careful when you're using it.

A natural comedian, Sagittarius often wastes time clowning around when he should be getting on with the work. Should he see a neighbour peering over the hedge at the brick wall he's building, he hops onto the top course and does a tightrope walk to the end. From which he falls into the cement mixer.

Though falling into the cement mixer is the best part of the act, the Sagittarian doesn't do it on purpose. He's accident prone, nearly as badly as Aries, and he shouldn't be let loose where he can do himself a mischief.

He's vulnerable in the shoulders, arms, hands, lungs, liver, hips and feet. His DIY projects are often delayed while he recovers from the damage he's done to one, more or all of them.

He is given to sweeping gestures, which is about all the sweeping he does, so be careful when he's showing you around.

'Just look at this,' he says, swiping wildly in the direction of a garden statue of Venus de Milo which he's plonked on a plinth with only a dab of cement. 'Isn't she – whoops!'

As he struggles to lift Venus off your shattered body, and you lie there in no fit condition to appreciate the lady's finer points, you could be forgiven for wishing that he was as armless.

('armless. Geddit? A do-it-yourself joke, that is. Was . . .)

Leaving Venus where she lies, to be restored to her plinth in another six months or so, Sagittarius strides purposefully across the lawn to show you the patio he's built. Or half built. After he's tripped over the only course of stone he's laid, it's your turn to pick *him* up.

Within a couple of years, the house is a shambles and the garden looks like a scale model of the Somme. But the Sagittarian doesn't let little things like that bother him. With his eyes on the far horizon and a dozen other schemes buzzing around in his head, he's got the perfect answer.

He moves.

CAPRICORN
(December 21 – January 19)

Careful, plodding, tenacious Capricorn is just the opposite of the loony Sagittarian.

The most ambitious and successful sign of the Zodiac, Capricorn's life is devoted to betterment of self and surroundings. All hobbies are practical ones – never mind the enjoyment, they must show an end result – and holidays are often spent working around the house.

It's not only the sense of achievement that appeals to Capricorn; it's also the money that's saved. A Capricorn wallet or purse is opened so seldom that the portraits on the notes start blinking in the light and sneezing in the dust.

Capricorn is never in a hurry. Meticulous work and steady progress on a long-term basis, that's the secret. As the work progresses, every detail is double-checked and every penny spent is accounted for. And when something is built, it stays built: no walls collapse, no bookshelves fall down, no doors drop from their hinges. There's no fussiness, no decoration for the sake of it. Whatever Capricorn produces is solid and simple. (Whoever shouted 'Boring!' can stay behind at four o'clock.)

Capricorn tools are always clean, shining and ready for use on orderly racks. They are never blunted, bent or broken by unskilled hands, because no unskilled hands ever get to use them. Capricorn is never a borrower, and is certainly no lender. Break your own tools.

Because of the sign's own high standards, Capricorn is impatient with anybody who does not achieve perfection and is hypercritical of others' work as well as his or her own. You can have advice on where you've gone wrong, but that's as far as it goes. You got yourself into that mess: get yourself out of it.

Capricorn himself is built to last, with strong hands and feet, and capable of great feats of endurance, working steadily away into the night until a job is finished.

But, tough though he is, he's not indestructible. The sign is vulnerable in the joints and bones, and prone to broken arms and legs. The breaks do not come about because of Capricorn's carelessness: more than likely because Aries or Sagittarius flings open the door and barges in without so much as – Aaaarrrrgh!

Stomach disorders can set in, caused either by fretting over the jobs or by eating incompatible foods during hastily snatched breaks.

In extreme cases of worry, psychosomatic paralysis may set in: Nature's way of telling you that you're fed up to the back teeth with the job.

Skin is sensitive, too, prone to allergies and nervous rashes. There's also trouble caused by sweating, enlarged pores and acne. Which may lead to the tactless Sagittarian greeting of, 'Morning, Cap'n! How's your belly off for spots?'

Not that Sagittarius had much chance before, but if he thinks he's going to borrow tools after *that* . . .

AQUARIUS
(January 20 – February 18)

If your own DIY skills leave a lot to be desired, cultivate an Aquarian. A friend of all the world, he is. Always taking on other people's burdens. Always doing good turns. Always willing to pitch in with practical help. Totally unable to refuse anybody a favour. A sucker if ever there was one.

What's more, Aquarius works best on his own. So once he's putting his back into laying your concrete, you're doing *him* a good turn by clearing off to the pub. Don't want to get in his way.

Aquarius is fascinated by new technology and loves to try out all the latest tools and labour saving devices. He tends not to have the tools long before they're borrowed. He'll lend them even when his need is greater than the cadger standing on the doorstep.

'Keep it as long as you like, old boy,' are Aquarius' parting words. And the cadger keeps it far longer than he should, only bringing it back to complain that this powered gribble dibbler is no good. Useless. In other words, broken. Bust. Kaput.

Aquarius wastes no words on recrimination. Does not even take the cadger to task for using the gribble dibbler to dibble a solid steel girder instead of the much softer gribble it was designed to dibble. Instead, he painstakingly takes the gribble dibbler apart to see if he can track down the design fault which caused the wobble which made the dibbler dobble.

He loves to know how everything works. Loves tinkering, taking things apart. The difference between him and some of the other signs is that he knows how to put things back.

The Aquarian mind is that of the original thinker, the inventor. He designs his own furniture and fittings and is quite capable of modifying tools to get the results he wants. Now and again he has to improvise because he's not very methodical and is often at a loss to remember where he put a particular tool, perhaps forgetting that six months ago he lent it to the cack-handed botcher next door.

Physically he's usually quite fit, but can suffer from circulation problems, sometimes brought on by bending double for too long over little finicky jobs. this is where his layabout neighbour is actually doing him a favour by involving him in more strenuous operations.

One thing never to involve Aquarius in, though, is shopping. His mind is often elsewhere, on another planet, busy with his next batch of dreams and ideas. So if you send him out for six 4-inch nails, a claw hammer and a sander, he's likely to come back with four 6-inch nails, a sledgehammer and a bandsaw. Oh, and a left-handed apple corer, a bicycle pump and three coconuts.

You didn't want a left-handed apple corer, a bicycle pump and three coconuts? Funny. Who *was* it the other day came round trying to borrow a left-handed apple corer, a bicycle pump and three coconuts . . . ?

PISCES (February 19 – March 20)

It's hard to know where to start with Pisces, if only for the reason that he often doesn't know whether he's coming or going, and sometimes isn't even sure where he's been. It's easy to follow his progress in DIY activities, though: just stumble through the mess of discarded tools from one pile of wreckage to the other.

Pisces is a scruffier operator even than Sagittarius, starts even more projects and gives them up much earlier.

He's a dreamer, you see. Not a visionary like Aquarius, or a crusader like Sagittarius, but a dreamer who wanders in a fantasy world to escape the realities around him.

He is often called aimless, impractical, bone idle and lacking in responsibility. This is the kind of harsh judgement that Scorpio would make, and would have no foundation in fact if Pisces weren't so aimless, impractical, bone idle and lacking in responsibility.

His is a water sign, symbolised by two fish swimming in opposite directions – even they don't know whether they're coming or going – and often signifies an interest in liquids. The liquids could be oil, water or chemicals, and he could be an expert in these fields. Oil, water and chemicals, however, are not the stuff that dreams are

made of, so Pisces often turns to liquids more conducive to reverie and becomes a drunk.

A characteristic attitude is standing with the legs crossed in an unconscious imitation of a fish's tail, which can be an indication that he's dreaming again. If he's standing there with crossed legs, pained expression, watering eyes and clutching his vitals, it's an indication that he's walked dreamily into something he left lying about.

He often relies on his partner to provide strength, purpose and a sense of direction. But even when strength, purpose and a sense of direction have been provided – 'When you've finished your meal, get out there and do something with that garden' – there's still no guarantee that any of it will survive longer than the first desultory prods with a fork.

One reason for the lack of staying power is that Pisces feels the onset of illness before anyone else. The slightest exertion can bring on his bad back. Just the thought of exertion can bring him out in a cold sweat.

He often stays at home for holidays: not so much because he can't tear himself away from the place, but because he can't make up his mind where to go.

For all his faults, Pisces is a pleasant, sociable character with an insatiable desire to help others. Should your Piscean neighbour see you struggling with a barrowload of bricks, he'll be the first to rush across to offer a hand. (Instead of rushing, he may lurch, stumble or stagger, but it's the thought that counts.)

The best thing you can do, if Pisces is not to wreck the place or do himself a mischief, is to put the barrow down and pretend you've finished for the day.

Remember that Pisces is sensitive and easily hurt, so don't just rush into the house, lock the doors and make noises like there's nobody home. That could upset him. Drive him to drink, even.

CHAPTER FOURTEEN

Famous Last Words and a Few Moving Epitaphs

Nothing sets the seal on a good, useful, colourful or heroic life like some Famous Last Words.

Who can forget, for instance, Charles II's 'Let not poor Nelly starve'. In his last moments he was doing a favour for Nell Gwynn, who had done him a favour or two in her time. Or Admiral Nelson's touching, 'Kiss me, Hardy'? Even if it did set his detractors saying, 'So it's true what we heard, then?'

Some went out fighting, like Britain's King George V who, on being advised to go to Bognor for his health, is said to have replied, 'Bugger Bognor'. And some went out prematurely, like General John Sedgwick, during the American Civil War battle of Spotsylvania. Peering over the parapet at the enemy, he said confidently, 'They couldn't hit an elephant at this dist –'

Do-it-yourselfers are renowned for their Famous Last Words, although, like those of poor old General Sedgwick, they tend to be a bit on the premature side.

'You don't need scaffolding for this job. Look – bucket on kitchen stool. Kitchen stool on tea trolley. Tea trolley on packing case. Packing case on garden table. Safe as –'

'I'm not paying an electrician to do a little job like this. All it needs is for the end of *this* wire to be twisted round the end of *this* –'

'Electric leads under these joists? Rubbish. I know the location of every wire in this –'

'I know the pane's a bit too big, but glass is a lot stronger and more flexible than people think. Just one firm shove and –'

'Four-by-three timber for this job would cost a fortune. Two-by-two is all I'm using. This will still be standing when I'm –'

'If I *had* tied these ladders at the top, I wouldn't be able to reach over to this –'

'Cat ladder on the roof? I've got perfect balance and co-ordination. Who needs –'

'Slippery up here? Of course it's slippery. But I'm wearing my supergrip wellies. You could walk up a brick wall in –'

'I *know* it's getting dark. But I can see the mower cable perfectly well. I'm going to finish this lawn tonight if it –'

'Yes, I *have* turned it off. Yes, it *has* stopped revolving. Out of my way while I –'

'Too many people are scared of gas. If you can find a leak before the build-up, you're as safe as houses. Why, you can even strike a –'

'Don't bother stacking those old bricks up there. Just throw them down to –'

'Load-bearing wall? This place is built like a tank. Why, I could knock out the whole of this –'

'Don't tell *me* about electrical colour codes. I was changing plugs before you were –'

'Put the guard on that power saw? If I do that it'll take all day to –'

'Rupture myself? Think I don't know how to lift? Of course I won't rup –'

'Nothing wrong with these ladders. My old dad used 'em for thirty –'

Last words might be the last from the Dear Departeds, but they're seldom the last words *about* them. A few other people – next-of-kin, insurance companies, banks, credit companies, mates they borrowed a few quid from – generally have a few things to say.

The last words of all are usually those inscribed on the tombstone, to which the deceased has every right of reply. As however, in the absence of a good medium, he often lacks the ability, what is inscribed on the stone is what posterity remembers him by.

The epitaphs of do-it-yourselfers need little or no explanation. You can picture the events which led to the premature demises and fill in your own backgrounds to the last stark chapters in the individual and unsung tragedies:

Here lies Arthur,
Willing and able.
Until he sawed through
That lost mains cable.

Here lies Herbert,
Out of puff.
He never knew
When he'd done enuff.

Here lies Dick,
Smart and slick,
'Til the chainsaw cut him
To the quick.

Here lies Joe.
They called him slow.
'Til he put that power drill
Through his toe.

Up leapt Pat,
Lithe as a cat,
'Til from the roof
He came down splat . . .

Here lies Sidney,
Feeling licked.
That unseen bucket
Was the last he kicked.

'I'll do it,' said Tim, feeling frisky.
'Don't nobody tell me it's risky.
'I'll knock down this wall.
'No trouble at all.'
At the funeral they went, 'Tssky-tssky . . .'

The job puzzled Fred
'Til he scratched his head
With a drill still running –
And now he's not funning.

What goes up
Must come down.
They're waiting for Harry
All over town.

Don't ask Jim
What became of him.
They put what was left
In the off-cuts bin.

Here lies Roddy,
Silly old soddy.
He kept his head,
But not his body.

Albert's thoughts were
Far from clear,
'Til he stuck a blowtorch
In his ear.
'Eureka! I've got it!'
He cried with delight,
Far too late
To see the light.

Here lies Benny
From Kilkenny,
Foe to none
And friend to many.
But the blast
Saw the last
Of most of Benny.
And not a lot more
Of old Kilkenny.

. . . Moving stuff, isn't it? And it leaves us with a moral, of which it behoves us all to take heed:

You can botch all your life,
Be a hell of a faker.
But nobody fools
The undertaker.